First World War
and Army of Occupation
War Diary
France, Belgium and Germany

7 INDIAN (MEERUT) DIVISION
Headquarters, Branches and Services
Commander Royal Artillery
1 June 1915 - 30 June 1915

WO95/3933/6

The Naval & Military Press Ltd
www.nmarchive.com
Published in association with The National Archives

Published by

The Naval & Military Press Ltd

Unit 10 Ridgewood Industrial Park,

Uckfield, East Sussex,

TN22 5QE England

Tel: +44 (0) 1825 749494

www.naval-military-press.com

www.nmarchive.com

This diary has been reprinted in facsimile from the original. Any imperfections are inevitably reproduced and the quality may fall short of modern type and cartographic standards.

© Crown Copyright
Images reproduced by permission of The National Archives, London, England, 2015.

Contents

Document type	Place/Title	Date From	Date To
Heading	Meerut Division H.Q. Div. Artillery From 1st to 30th June 1915		
Heading	War Diary of With Appendices Headquarters Divisional Artillery Meerut Division From 1st June 1915 To 30th June 1915		
War Diary	La Croix Marmeuse	01/06/1915	19/06/1915
War Diary	La Croix Barbee	19/06/1915	19/06/1915
War Diary	La Croix Marmeuse	20/06/1915	30/06/1915
Miscellaneous	Tactical Progress Report	01/06/1915	01/06/1915
Miscellaneous	Positions And Arc's Covered By 9'2" Howitzers 6" Guns & 60 Pr Batteries		
Miscellaneous	Tactical Progress Report	02/06/1915	02/06/1915
Miscellaneous	A Form Messages And Signals		
Miscellaneous	Appendix 234	03/06/1915	03/06/1915
Miscellaneous	Tactical Progress Report	03/06/1915	03/06/1915
Miscellaneous	No. G-116 Headquarters Meerut Division	03/06/1915	03/06/1915
Miscellaneous	Headquarters Divisional Artillery Meerut Division	03/06/1915	03/06/1915
Miscellaneous	Tactical Progress Report	04/06/1915	04/06/1915
Miscellaneous	Liason Barrages Meerut Divisional Artillery	04/06/1915	04/06/1915
Miscellaneous	A Form Messages And Signals		
Miscellaneous	Tactical Progress Report	05/06/1915	05/06/1915
Miscellaneous	Tactical Progress Report	06/06/1915	06/06/1915
Miscellaneous	Tactical Progress Report	07/06/1915	07/06/1915
Miscellaneous	Tactical Progress Report	08/06/1915	08/06/1915
Miscellaneous	A Form Messages And Signals		
Miscellaneous	Headquarters Divisional Artillery Meerut Division	08/06/1915	08/06/1915
Diagram etc	Diagram		
Miscellaneous	Tactical Progress Report	09/06/1915	09/06/1915
Miscellaneous	A Form Messages And Signals		
Miscellaneous	Tactical Progress Report	10/06/1915	10/06/1915
Miscellaneous	Headquarters Divisional Artillery Meerut Division	10/06/1915	10/06/1915
Miscellaneous	Tactical Progress Report	11/06/1915	11/06/1915
Miscellaneous	Tactical Progress Report	12/06/1915	12/06/1915
Miscellaneous	Tactical Progress Report	13/06/1915	13/06/1915
Miscellaneous	Tactical Progress Report	14/06/1915	14/06/1915
Miscellaneous	Extract from Indian Corps Operation Order No. 71 of 11/6/15	11/06/1915	11/06/1915
Miscellaneous	Extract from Indian Corps Operation Order No. 71 dated 11th June 1915 received under cover Meerut Division No G-339 dated the 11th June 1915	11/06/1915	11/06/1915
Miscellaneous	Headquarters Meerut Division	11/06/1915	11/06/1915
Miscellaneous	Headquarters Divisional Artillery Meerut Division	12/06/1915	12/06/1915
Miscellaneous	Headquarters Meerut Division	13/06/1915	13/06/1915
Miscellaneous	A Form Messages And Signals		
Miscellaneous	OC 13th Brigade RFA	14/06/1915	14/06/1915
Miscellaneous	Meerut Division	14/06/1915	14/06/1915
Miscellaneous	Headquarters Divisional Artillery Meerut Division	14/06/1915	14/06/1915
Miscellaneous	Headquarters Meerut Division	14/06/1915	14/06/1915
Miscellaneous	O.C. 13th Brigade R.F.A.	14/06/1915	14/06/1915
Miscellaneous	Tactical Progress Report	15/06/1915	15/06/1915

Miscellaneous	A Form Messages And Signals		
Miscellaneous	Tactical Progress Report	16/06/1915	16/06/1915
Miscellaneous	Tactical Progress Report	17/06/1915	17/06/1915
Miscellaneous	A Form Messages And Signals		
Miscellaneous	Tactical Progress Report	18/06/1915	18/06/1915
Miscellaneous	4th Corps & Attached Artillery Instructions No.8	18/06/1915	18/06/1915
Miscellaneous	Tactical Progress Report	19/06/1915	19/06/1915
Miscellaneous	A Form Messages And Signals		
Miscellaneous	Tactical Progress Report	20/06/1915	20/06/1915
Miscellaneous	A Form Messages And Signals		
Miscellaneous	Tactical Progress Report	21/06/1915	21/06/1915
Miscellaneous	4th Corps Artillery Instructions No.9	21/06/1915	21/06/1915
Miscellaneous	Headquarters Divisional Artillery Meerut Division	21/06/1915	21/06/1915
Miscellaneous	Tactical Progress Report	22/06/1915	22/06/1915
Operation(al) Order(s)	Operation Order No. 39 Sir By Lieutenant-General /C.A. Anderson, K.C.B. Commanding Meerut Division.	23/06/1915	23/06/1915
Miscellaneous	Appendix 277	23/06/1915	23/06/1915
Miscellaneous	Appendix 278	23/06/1915	23/06/1915
Miscellaneous	Tactical Progress Report	23/06/1915	23/06/1915
Miscellaneous	Tactical Progress Report	24/06/1915	24/06/1915
Miscellaneous	Tactical Progress Report	25/06/1915	25/06/1915
Operation(al) Order(s)	Operation Order No.40 By Lieutenant General Sir C.A. Anderson, K.C.B. Commanding Meerut Division	25/06/1915	25/06/1915
Miscellaneous	Headquarters Divisional Artillery Meerut Division	25/06/1915	25/06/1915
Miscellaneous	Tactical Progress Report	26/06/1915	26/06/1915
Miscellaneous	Tactical Progress Report	27/06/1915	27/06/1915
Operation(al) Order(s)	Operation Order No. 41 By Lieutenant-General Sir Charles Anderson, K.C.B. Commanding Meerut Division	27/06/1915	27/06/1915
Miscellaneous	Operation Order No. 41 By Lieutenant-General Sir Charles Anderson, K.C.B. Commanding Meerut Division	27/06/1915	27/06/1915
Miscellaneous	Headquarters Divisional Artillery Meerut Division	28/06/1915	28/06/1915
Miscellaneous	Tactical Progress Report	28/06/1915	28/06/1915
Miscellaneous	Tactical Progress Report	29/06/1915	29/06/1915
Miscellaneous	Headquarters Divisional Artillery Meerut Division	30/06/1915	30/06/1915
Miscellaneous	Meerut Divisional Artillery	30/06/1915	30/06/1915
Miscellaneous	Tactical Progress Report	30/06/1915	30/06/1915

Meerut Division

H. Q. Div. Artillery.

From 1st To 30th June 1915

Serial No. 65.

121/6128

WAR DIARY

with Appendices.

Head Quarters, Divisional Artillery, Meerut Division.

From 1st June 1915 to 30th June 1915.

Army Form C. 2118.

VOLUME XI

WAR DIARY
INTELLIGENCE SUMMARY.
(Erase heading not required.)

Hour, Date, Place		Summary of Events and Information	Remarks and references to Appendices
4.5.a.m. 1st June 1915 LA CROIX MARMEUSE		19th Battery, from new position, registered FERME du BOIS, Ferme COUR d'AVOUE and DISTILLERY.	
4.30.a.m.	do......	14th Battery registered new trench J.15-K.7, also points K.6. and J.12. Bursts of fire were maintained on this trench throughout the day in accordance with instructions received from the 1st Army.	× Appendix 231(a)
5.a.m.	do......	28th Battery, from new position, registered DISTILLERY, Q.8., M.16., M.20.,K.12., P.14.; and german front trench opposite P.11 to LA QUINQUE RUE- two direct hits on P.14.	
6.a.m.	do......	66th Battery registered the following points with aeroplane: E.28.a.4'2 - L.17. - S.29.c.5'5. 7th Battery registered K.8.-J.18 North and South ends of trench in A 3 b.	×Appendix 232
9.a.m.	do......	Neighbourhood of the 14th Battery was shelled by PIPSQUEAK for about an hour.	
9.45.a.m.	do......	2nd Battery fired in german trenches in retaliation.	
3.p.m.;3.25.p.m. and 3.35.p.m 3.45.p.m			
12.25.p.m.	do......	PIPSQUEAK shelled trenches between P.10 and Q.7.	
2.20.p.m.	do......	2nd Battery fired on enemy working party near V.2.	
3.p.m.	do......	8th Battery registered house Q.11 and Redoubt near Q.15.	
3.15.p.m.	do......	PIPSQUEAKS were falling 50 yards in rear of 66th Battery in salvoes of three's. Appeared to come from LORGIES. This battery was also searching and sweeping country between 66th Battery position and RICHEBOURG. Retort on S.29.a.9'0 claimed to have silenced them, but report from another source located the flashes at S 23 c 9'9.	
3.20.p.m.	do......	2nd Battery engaged PIPSQUEAK Battery located at S 23 c 9'9 which was shelling RICHEBOURG, in co-operation with 48th Heavy Battery- fire was reported as very effective.	
5.p.m.	do......	19th Battery registered the following points by aeroplane:- N.23., M.20., M.12., and trench at centre of S.28. 44th Battery carriedour registration during the morning. 66th Battery registered M.13-M.11.	

For further information see Tactical Progress Report attached.
Points shelled and arcs covered by 9'2" Howitzer, 6" guns and 60 pr. Batteries is shown in Appendix 233 attached

*Appendix 232
ØAppendix 233

Army Form...

WAR DIARY
or
INTELLIGENCE SUMMARY.
(Erase heading not required.)

Instructions regarding War Diaries and Intelligence Summaries are contained in F.S. Regs., Part II. and the Staff Manual respectively. Title pages will be prepared in manuscript.

Hour, Date, Place	Summary of Events and Information	Remarks and references to Appendices
1st June 1915. LA CROIX MARMEUSE.	No.1 Group H.A.R. having been moved SOUTH, and only the 1st and 4th Brigades R.G.A. were left in this area. Headquarters 1st Brigade R.G.A. at VEILLE CHAPELLE with telephonic communication direct with Headquarters Divisional artillery, MEERUT DIVISION at LA CROIX MARMEUSE. All work by heavy Counter Batteries carried out by 1st Brigade R.G.A. to whom all communications are made.	

(9 29 6) W 4141—463 100,000 9/14 H W V Forms/C. 2118/10

Army Form C. 211b.

WAR DIARY
or
INTELLIGENCE SUMMARY.
(*Erase heading not required.*)

Instructions regarding War Diaries and Intelligence Summaries are contained in F.S. Regs., Part II. and the Staff Manual respectively. Title pages will be prepared in manuscript.

Hour, Date, Place	Summary of Events and Information	Remarks and references to Appendices
1st June 1915.......... LA CROIX MARMEUSE.	Location of MEERUT Divisional Artillery as follows:-	
	Headquarters MEERUT Division........R 15 d 4 9.	
	Headquarters Divisional Artillery......R 21 c 2 4. MEERUT DIVISION.	
	Headquarters 4th Brigade R.F.A.........M 26 o 5 1.	
	7th Battery R.F.A..........S 20 c 3 7.	
	14th Battery R.F.A..........S 20 c 8 3.	
	66th Battery R.F.A..........S 2 d 5 2.	
	Headquarters 9th Brigade R.F.A.........X 17 d 7 7.	
	19th Battery R.F.A..........S 7 b 1 7.	
	20th Battery R.F.A..........X 18 a 4 4.	
	28th Battery R.F.A..........X 24 a 9 5.	
	Headquarters 13th Brigade R.F.A.........M 31 b 4 3.	
	2nd Battery R.F.A..........M 32 a 2 7.	
	8th Battery R.F.A..........M 31 b 9 7.	
	44th Battery R.F.A..........M 31 d 5 6.	
	30th Howitzer Battery R.F.A......S 7 b 2 10.	
	Headquarters MEERUT Divisional Ammn Col R 26 a 7 6.	

Forms/C. 2118/10

(9 22 6) W 4141—463 100,000 9/14 H W V

Army Form C. 2118.

WAR DIARY
or
INTELLIGENCE SUMMARY.
(Erase heading not required.)

Instructions regarding War Diaries and Intelligence Summaries are contained in F.S. Regs., Part II. and the Staff Manual respectively. Title pages will be prepared in manuscript.

Hour, Date, Place	Summary of Events and Information	Remarks and references to Appendices
10.30.a.m. 2nd June 1915. LA CROIX MARMEUSE.	19th Battery registered M.30., and N.23., to verify observation carried out with aeroplane yesterday.	
11.a.m.	44th Battery fired on normal lines.	
11.30.a.m.	20th Battery registered trench running S.W. from P.14. the parapet of which has been strengthened during the night, and obtained direct hits on M.11.,M.12.,M.14.,M.15.,M.16. 19th Battery registered the FERME du TOULOTTE.	
11.35.a.m.	PIPSQUEAK shelled the vicinity of LEICESTER LOUNGE.	
11.45.a.m. and } 2.15.p.m. } 4.23.p.m. }	2nd Battery fired on enemy's trenches in retaliation.	apparently 15&
1.p.m.	8th Battery registered 44th Battery's front Q.8-Q.7 and trench 100 yards S. of P.17.	
2.45.p.m.	28th Battery registered points P.28.,N.23., and M.20.	
3.37.p.m.	2nd Battery registered trench near Q.15.	
4.p.m.	8th Battery registered trench Q.16 where work had been done during the night.	
6.45.p.m.	20th Battery registered enemy's support trench opposite P.10 to P.11.	
8.30.p.m.	Heavy howitzer from direction of midway between BEAU PUITS and VIOLAINES dropped 15 shell over right flank reserve trenches of the BAREILLY Brigade.	
	30th Howitzer Battery carried out registration. "Mother" was turn on to PIPSQUEAK Batteries at S.30.a.5'1 and S.25.c.9'9, which had been troublesome during the past few days- hits were obtained and batteries silenced. CHOCOLAT MENIER CORNER and vicinity was shelled by PIPSQUEAK at intervals during the day. 44th Battery moved to new position at M 32 o 10&7. For further information see Tactical Progress Report attached.	* Appendix 234

Army Form C. 2118.

WAR DIARY
or
INTELLIGENCE SUMMARY.
(Erase heading not required.)

Instructions regarding War Diaries and Intelligence Summaries are contained in F.S. Regs., Part II. and the Staff Manual respectively. Title pages will be prepared in manuscript.

Hour, Date, Place	Summary of Events and Information	Remarks and references to Appendices
8.a.m. 3rd June 1915. LA CROIX MARMEUSE.	GORRE WOOD vicinity and "Tuning Fork" road shelled by 21.c.m. Howitzer.	
8.43.a.m. to 11.40.a.m.	2nd Battery fired on enemy's trenches in retaliation for PIPSQUEAK firing at trench near V.l.	
9.a.m. do.	15.c.m. howitzer shelled our support trenches near Q.6.	
9.10.a.m. do.	PIPSQUEAK shelled trenches in vicinity of P.10.	
9.10.a.m. do.	20th Battery registered communication trench leading from E. of P.11 to german front trench.	
9.15.a.m. do.	2nd Battery registered point on german trench 50 yards S.of R.8.	
10.55.a.m. and 12.25.p.m. do.	2nd Battery fired on PIPSQUEAK Battery which was subsequently engaged effectively by 48th Heavy Battery with observation from "LEICESTER LOUNGE (S.9.d.3.6)	* Appendix 13y
11.30.a.m. and 6.10.p.m. do.	44th Battery registered from new position in M 32 c 10'7 occupied last night, old position vacated owing to being located by Germans.	
11.35.a.m. do.	8th Siege Battery fired one round at battery which was active from N 33 e 1'3 -48th Heavy Battery then took it on.	
12 noon. do.	Heavy howitzer and PIPSQUEAK shelled communication trench from P.5. to OLD BRITISH LINE and also on reserve trenches from direction of BEAU PUITS.	
12.15.p.m. do.	PIPSQUEAK and Heavy Howitzer shelled our trenches in vicinity P.10.	
12.25.p.m. do.	8th Siege Battery fired two rounds at T 10 c 2'0 (WARNETON) - no activity seen so ceased firing.	
12.30.p.m. do.	15.c.m. howitzer shelled vicinity S 19 d and road 200 yards W.of BREWERY (S 20 c 9'1).	
1.30.p.m. do.	PIPSQUEAK shelled new trench P.10 to LA QUINQUE RUE, also communication trench and present fire trench P.10-P.9-N.11.	
2.15.p.m. do.	8th Battery fired at a house about M.20-which appears to be used as am O.P.	
3.p.m. do.	21.c.m. howitzer shelled vicinity our front trenches about P.10 from direction of LORGIES.	
4.10.p.m. do.	8th Battery fired at trench R.8-Q.15. in retaliation for shelling our own trenches.	
4.30.p.m. do.	10.5.c.m. howitzer shelled vicinity X 17 d 9'3.	
6.25.p.m. do.	8th Siege Battery fired 6 rounds at hostile battery whose flashes were observed at A 6 b 4'0. FESTUBERT was shelled from direction of VIOLAINES.	

Army Form C. 2118.

WAR DIARY
or
INTELLIGENCE SUMMARY.
(Erase heading not required.)

Instructions regarding War Diaries and Intelligence Summaries are contained in F. S. Regs., Part II. and the Staff Manual respectively. Title pages will be prepared in manuscript.

Hour, Date, Place	Summary of Events and Information	Remarks and references to Appendices
4.p.m. to 6.p.m. 3rd June LA CROIX MARMEUSE.	3 batteries of 4th Brigade R.F.A. co-operated with operations of the 4th Corps by slow continuous bombardment of (-50 rds per battery):- (i) L.17-trench junction S 28 a 3'5. (ii) K.13 "communication way" (iii) Vicinity L.11, L.12., L.13.	This was special tasks allotted to the 4th Brigade R.F.A. x Appendix 234(a) x Appendix 18th
7.p.m. to 8.p.m. do.......	A very slow rate of fire as mentioned on above tasks by request of 7th Divisional Artillery.	ø Appendix 234(b).
8.p.m. to 9.40.p.m. do....... 10.p.m. to 3.a.m. do....... 4/6/15	Above operation was repeated (50 rounds per battery). 1 Battery 4th Brigade fired occasional rounds every hour on L.17 and approaches. 1 Battery 4th Brigade fired similarly on vicinity K.11, K.12., K.13. Reference above see C.R.A. 59 ø.	* Appendix 235
9.20.p.m. do.......	2nd Battery retaliated on enemy's trenches at request of Infantry as our trenches were being badly PIPSQUEAKED. *	No.9 x appendix 235(b) * appendix 236(b)
	For further information see Tactical Progress Report attached. Received Divison No G.416 re research for economy in ammunition received and replied to under No 708 RA(h)*	

Army Form C. 2118.

WAR DIARY
or
INTELLIGENCE SUMMARY.
(Erase heading not required.)

Instructions regarding War Diaries and Intelligence Summaries are contained in F.S. Regs., Part II. and the Staff Manual respectively. Title pages will be prepared in manuscript.

Hour, Date, Place	Summary of Events and Information	Remarks and references to Appendices
9.55.a.m. 4th June 1915. LA CROIX MARMEUSE	2nd Battery fired at enemy's trenches in retaliation.	
10.30.a.m. do	21.c.m. howitzer shelled vicinity of X 18 c for about 1½ hours.	
11.a.m. do	8th Battery fired at trench R.8. where germans were seen.	
11.10.a.m. do	15.c.m. howitzer shelled house at S 21 o 9'3, mentioned as a likely ranging spot yesterday.	
11.15.a.m. do	20th Battery registered ORCHARD near P.18 and house between P.16 and Q.12.	
11.30.a.m. do	19th Battery registered trench Q.12—Q.15.	
11.45.a.m. do	15.c.m. howitzer shelled RICHEBOURG for about an hour, including 7th and 14th Battery's positions- direction of LORGIES indicated.	*Appendix 15*
12.15.p.m. do	Infantry reserve near N.2. shelled by howitzers from direction of DISTILLERY. PIPSQUEAK shelled vicinity of S 8 a. and S 7 b. PIPSQUEAK shelled CHOCOLAT MENIER CORNER (S 14 b 7'4).	
12.45.p.m. do	2nd Battery fired at farm near P.18. to check registration.	
1.4.p.m. do	St VAAST Post heavily shelled by heavy howitzers (15.c.m. ? 21.c.m.)- direction LORGIES.	
1.40.p.m. do	8th Siege Battery engaged T 19 c 2'9 in response to shelling of First Aid Post and S 2 c. Direct hit on house just over LORGIES Church at 2nd round.	
1.55.p.m. do	Above batteries again active, 8th Siege Battery fired 4 rounds of lyddite and batteries then ceased firing.	
2.30.p.m. do	PIPSQUEAK shelled reserve trenches East of INDIAN VILLAGE.	
3.p.m. do	15.c.m. howitzer shelled new communication trench N.11—P.11 from direction of LA RUSSIE- was silenced by 4th Brigade R.G.A.	
4.p.m. do	8th Battery registered on R.10 and FERME de TOULOTTE.	
4.30.p.m. do	21.c.m. howitzer shelled vicinity of S 8 a. 4'4.	
8.1.p.m. do	66th Battery, South of RICHEBOURG, shelled by PIPSQUEAKS from direction of VIOLAINES.	
5.50.p.m. do	2nd Battery registered house with 2 loopholes high up, at or near N.24, which is obviously an O.P.-visible from LEICESTER LOUNGE.	Appendix 236
10.p.m. do	A few PIPSQUEAKS falling in RICHEBOURG. For further information see Tactical Progress Report.*	*Appendix
	BARRAGES to be formed by the MEERUT Divisional Artillery is shown in Appx 237.	Appendix 237

Army Form C. 2118.

WAR DIARY
or
INTELLIGENCE SUMMARY.
(Erase heading not required.)

Instructions regarding War Diaries and Intelligence Summaries are contained in F.S. Regs., Part II. and the Staff Manual respectively. Title pages will be prepared in manuscript.

Hour, Date, Place	Summary of Events and Information	Remarks and references to Appendices
4th June 1915... LA CROIX MARMEUSE.	Lieut R.D. BEALL, 7th Battery R.F.A. was killed by a direct hit on Bomb Proof in the 7th Battery by 5'9" Howitzer shell. Headquarters 13th Brigade R.F.A. were moved to R 29 d 8'8 during the day on account of the constant shelling of their old headquarters 30th Howitzer Battery R.F.A. was replaced at the disposal of the O.C. 43rd Howitzer Brigade R.F.A. in accordance with MEERUT Division message No.G-164.×	× Appendix 238 (No.3)

Army Form C. 2118.

WAR DIARY
or
INTELLIGENCE SUMMARY.
(Erase heading not required.)

Instructions regarding War Diaries and Intelligence Summaries are contained in F.S. Regs., Part II. and the Staff Manual respectively. Title pages will be prepared in manuscript.

Hour, Date, Place	Summary of Events and Information	Remarks and references to Appendices
4.a.m. 5th June 1915. LA CROIX MARMEUSE.	RITZ and vicinity shelled by PIPSQUEAKS.	
4.45.a.m.	do. do.	
9.45.a.m.	19th Battery fired on working party at P.17 and disturbed them.	
12.noon.	21.c.m. howitzer shelled vicinity of X 18 a-firing about 6 rounds.	
2.10.p.m. to 3.30.p.m.)do. 4.30 to 4.45.p.m.)	Trenches in vicinity of M.8. were heavily shelled. At 4.45.p.m. fire was switched on to the ORCHARD(S 21 d). Infantry report these trenches badly damaged.	× Appendix 154.
3.p.m.	8th Battery registered earthworks near Q.18.	
3.45.p.m.	PIPSQUEAK shelled RUE del'EPINETTE. 15.c.m. howitzer shelled vicinity X 6 a for about 1½ hours.	
4.p.m.	10.5.c.m. howitzer shelled vicinity of X 18 c for a quarter of an hour.	
4.5.p.m.	2nd Battery registered N.27 suspected as being an O.P., as men seen leaving,wit and two horses grazing near.	
5.p.m.	10.5.c.m.(or 15.c.m.)howitzer shelled our front trenches in vicinity of S 21 b from direction of BOIS du BIEZ.	
5.30.p.m.	PIPSQUEAK shelled ORCHARD N.12-N.13-M.9 for considerable time.	
5.42.p.m.	MOTHER fired two rounds at LA RUSSIE battery "by request", owing to report of howitzer shelling "B" Sub-section trenches from that direction.	
6.25.p.m.	PIPSQUEAK shelled track from INDIAN VILLAGE S 20 a, to RUE de l'EPINETTE.	
6.30.p.m.	PIPSQUEAK shelled CHOCOLAT MENIER CORNER(S 14 b 7˙5).	
	44th Battery registered the FERME du TOULOTTE and FERME du BOIS during the day.	
	House N.24 reported in yesterday's Tactical Progress Report as likely O.P. was taken on to-day by MOTHER—1st round hit the corner and several germans were seen bolting— 2nd round just over— 3rd round plump into middle of the house.	
	* Orders were received from the 1st Army for one Brigade R.F.A.(9th Brigade) to be placed at the disposal of the 4th Corps temporarily for Tactical purposes. This Brigade will remain in its present position and cover the front of the BAREILLY Brigade until such time as the 4th Brigade R.F.A. have sufficiently registered to take over. "This "selection" of particular units by higher authority is strongly to be deprecated.	* Appendix 239.

Army Form C. 2118.

WAR DIARY
or
INTELLIGENCE SUMMARY.
(Erase heading not required.)

Instructions regarding War Diaries and Intelligence Summaries are contained in F.S. Regs., Part II. and the Staff Manual respectively. Title pages will be prepared in manuscript.

Hour, Date, Place	Summary of Events and Information	Remarks and references to Appendices
5th June 1915. LA CROIX MARMEUSE.	Information received from Indian Corps that one section of 4'5" Hows would be placed at the disposal of the MEERUT Division, together with proportion of ammunition column echelon from the 8th Division.	*Appendix 240.
	Information regarding the work carried out by the Heavy Artillery on the front of the MEERUT Division is shown in the daily Tactical Progress Report.	
	For further information see Tactical Progress Report attached.	∮ Appendix 241.
	Section of the 55th Howitzer Battery from the 8th Divisional Artillery joined the MEERUT Divisional Artillery and went into action after dark in position vacated by 30th Howitzer Battery at S 7 b 2˙10.	

(9 29 6) W 4141—463 100,000 9/14 H W V   Forms/C. 2118/10

Army Form C. 2118.

WAR DIARY
or
INTELLIGENCE SUMMARY.
(Erase heading not required.)

Instructions regarding War Diaries and Intelligence Summaries are contained in F.S. Regs., Part II. and the Staff Manual respectively. Title pages will be prepared in manuscript.

Hour, Date, Place	Summary of Events and Information	Remarks and references to Appendices
8.15.a.m. 6th June 1915. LA CROIX MARMEUSE.	2nd Battery fired at Germans seen near V.4.	
10.45.a.m.	10.5.c.m. howitzer shelled our support trenches in vicinity of N.9. from direction of VIOLAINES.	
11.30.a.m.	15.c.m. howitzer shelled vicinity S 19 d from direction of BEAU PUITS.	
1.p.m.	15.c.m. howitzer shelled vicinity of X 18 c. PIPSQUEAK and 10.5.c.m. howitzer shelled 1st and 2nd line trenches of "A" Sub-section. Fire was reported very accurate and was continued for considerable period, aeroplane reports battery at T 21 b as culprit.	*Appendix 13 to*
1.30.p.m.	20th Battery registered trench L.11-L.12 and all conspicuous points in vicinity of RUE d'OUVERT, also houses on road running towards M.8. and part of trench running out towards L.10.	
1.40.p.m.	19th Battery registered trenches in vicinity of L.12.	
2.40.p.m.	2nd Battery fired at suspected O.P.- N.27.	
2.45.p.m.	The 4th Brigade R.F.A. having reported that its batteries were now sufficiently registered on BAREILLY Brigade front to take up the Artillery support of this front, and communications having now been established with BAREILLY Brigade—with 2nd Highland Brigade R.F.A.(T.F.) on its right and with 13th Brigade R.F.A. on its left, also liaison between each battery and Infantry Battalion on allotted front, information was sent to MEERUT Division, 7th Divisional Artillery, BAREILLY Bde, HIGHLAND Divisional Artillery, that 4th Brigade had taken up responsibility of Artillery support of this front from 9th Brigade R.F.A. and that 9th Brigade R.F.A. was now placed at disposal of 4th Corps, in accordance with direct instructions of 1st Army.*	* Appendix 259.
2.46.p.m.	2nd Battery engaged PIPSQUEAK near S 25 c 9'9.	
5.p.m.	13th Brigade R.F.A. reported that 2nd 2nd Gurkhas had asked for Artillery fire on FERME cour d'AVOINE at 11.45.p.m. and 12.30.a.m. to disturb enemy working parties. MEERUT Division, LAHORE Divisional Artillery, Highland Divisional Artillery, 1st Brigade R.G.A., 4th and 9th Brigades R.F.A. informed that firing would take place. 28th Battery registered VIOLAINES, K.24, houses at L.15 and L.11, points L.12, M.14, K.12, trench L.11-L.13 L.10.	

Forms/C. 2118/10
(9 29 6) W 4141—463 100,000 9/14 H W V

Army Form C. 2118.

WAR DIARY
or
INTELLIGENCE SUMMARY.
(Erase heading not required.)

Instructions regarding War Diaries and Intelligence Summaries are contained in F.S. Regs., Part II. and the Staff Manual respectively. Title pages will be prepared in manuscript.

Hour, Date, Place	Summary of Events and Information	Remarks and references to Appendices
3.30.p.m. 6th June 1915. LA CROIX MARMEUSE.	8th Battery fired at trench 300 yards E. of FERME de TOULOTTE.	
4.55.p.m.& 5.15.p.m. do.	14th Battery fired 6 rounds on enemy's trenches in retaliation for our own trenches being shelled.	
4.55.p.m. do.	8th Battery fired two slavoes on trench R.8. to Q.16 in retaliation.	
5.30.p.m. do.	2nd, 8th, 14th, and 66th Batteries R.F.A. carried out combined shoot with MOTHER on house S.W. of Q.12— a few rounds only fired.	
5.45.p.m. do.	15.c.m. howitzer shelled vicinity X 18 a and cross roads X 18 c 10'7 for one hour and obtained direct hits on house X 18 c 10'8.	x appendix 258.
6.p.m. do.	2nd Battry fire to stop PIPSQUEAK at S 23 c 9'9 with good result.	
6.15.p.m. do.	14th Battery fired on german trenches as their Artillery fired on our support trenches.	
	Batteries of the 4th Brigade R.F.A. carried out registration during the day.	
	There were several "bursts" of hostile fire on our first line trench near P,10 during the afternoon.	
	4th Brigade R.F.A. had been especially put into action South of RICHEBOURG to cover front of 4th Corps and render it assistance during pending operations. It had registered various trenches near RUE d'OUVERT (and South of RUE du MARAIS with both aeroplane observation and visual observation. This is accordance with instructions of the Brigadier General, Royal Artillery, Indian Corps.	* Appendix 259.
	To-day these batteries had to carry out fresh registration on BAREILLY Brigade front, already thoroughly well registered by 9th Brigade R.F.A. in order to allow 9th Brigade to be placed at disposal of 4th Corps, in accordance with orders of the 1st Army. The 9th Brigade on the other hand had perforce to carry out fresh registration off its normal front, in order to be able to assist the 4th Corps during pending operations. A good deal of extra registration was thus entailed and consequent expenditure of ammunition.	∮ Appendix 257(a).
	For daily Tactical Progress Report see Appendix	Appendix 242

Army Form C. 2118.

WAR DIARY
or
INTELLIGENCE SUMMARY.
(Erase heading not required.)

Instructions regarding War Diaries and Intelligence Summaries are contained in F.S. Regs., Part II. and the Staff Manual respectively. Title pages will be prepared in manuscript.

Hour, Date, Place	Summary of Events and Information	Remarks and references to Appendices
8.a.m. & 17th June 1915. LA CROIX MARMEUSE.	66th Battery fired on trenches near FERME COUR d'AVOINE in retaliation to enemy's batteries shelling our trenches.	
11.25.a.m.	Enemy's PIPSQUEAK searched up to 50 yds of 7th Battery new position at S 21 a 0.7, fragments coming into the battery- no damage.	
9.45.a.m. (to)		
10.45.a.m.		
10.45.a.m. do	PIPSQUEAK Battery hit 14th Battery O.P. and a little later hit houses close to O.P. Very active in this locality (CHOCOLATE MENIER CORNER).	Appendix 154
10.12.a.m. do	15.c.m. Howitzer shelled vicinity X 18 c- a few rounds only.	
11.a.m. do	14th Battery fired on enemy's trenches in retaliation to enemy's batteries firing on our trenches.	
11.15.a.m. do	44th Battery fired at points near FERME COUR d'AVOINE and at ruins indicated by and at request of O.C. 2nd 2nd Gurkhas.	
12.30.p.m. do	PIPSQUEAK shelled BREWERY Roads (S 20 c).	
1.p.m. do	14th Battery fired at working party near P.14.	
	44th Battery registered farm on RUE du MARAIS and two localities S.E. of FERME COUR d'AVOINE.	
1.45.p.m. do	15.c.m. howitzer shelled vicinity X 18 c for about half an hour.	
4.15.p.m. do	66th Battery registered trench S 28 a 2.9 to S 28 a 9.9.	
4.30.p.m. do	8th Battery completed registration on trench at R.10.	
5.p.m. do	8th Battery fired a few rounds at DOLL's HOUSE-N.27 (a probable O.P.)	
	7th Battery carried out registration from its new position, following points being registered:- J.20, K.7, K.12, A 4 a 8.7, S 28 a 5.6, S 29 c 5.4. Section of the 55th Howitzer Battery carried out registration during the day, with percussion shrapnel. During the morning PIPSQUEAK and 10.5.c.m. Howitzer shelled our trenches in vicinity S 15 intermittently.	
	For further information see Tactical Progress Report attached.	*Appendix 243

Army Form C. 2118.

WAR DIARY
or
INTELLIGENCE SUMMARY.
(Erase heading not required.)

Instructions regarding War Diaries and Intelligence Summaries are contained in F.S. Regs., Part II. and the Staff Manual respectively. Title pages will be prepared in manuscript.

Hour, Date, Place	Summary of Events and Information	Remarks and references to Appendices
6.30.a.m. 8th June 1915. LA CROIX MARMEUSE.	PIPSQUEAK shelled in front of 14th and 66th Batteries (South of RICHEBOURG).	
6.45.a.m. and) 12.5.p.m.)	14th Battery fired a few rounds on enemy's trenches in retaliation to enemy shelling ours.	
11.15.a.m. do	66th Battery fired on enemy's trenches in reply to PIPSQUEAK firing on our reserve trenches.	
1.50.p.m. do	8th Battery fired on R.8. - Q.16. in retaliation.	
2.p.m. do	2nd Battery fired on night lines in retaliation.	
2.15.p.m. do	2nd Battery fired to stop enemy bombing our trenches near V.2. Bombing ceased.	Appendix 134.
4.20.p.m. and) do	2nd Battery registered V.3. to R.8. as new night line.	
5.40.p.m.) do		
5.30.p.m. do	PIPSQUEAK shelled INDIAN VILLAGE (S.20).	
5.50.p.m. do	PIPSQUEAK active on roads in S 2 c.	
6.p.m. do	PIPSQUEAK shelled vicinity L.18 a and X 18 c.	
5.30.p.m. to) do	7th Battery registered L.11 - L.12 and Salient to West.	
6.30.p.m.)		
6.45.p.m. do	PIPSQUEAK fired a few shell N.W. of RICHEBOURG.	
	Section of 55th Howitzer Battery registered FERME du BOIS and trench in front, also farm near P.18 during the day.	
	HIGHLAND Division trenches throughout the day, as a result of their bombardment of enemy trenches and wire.	
	Work carried out by the 1st and 4th Brigades R.G.A., with information on other points, will be found in the Tactical Progress Report* which * Appendix 244. is attached.	
	Indian Corps asked for details of excess in expenditure of ammunition on the 7th instant, this was furnished to the MEERUT Division (see Appendices 245 and 246)	Appendices 245 & 246.
	Panorama view from LEICESTER LOUNGE by 2nd Lieut D.C. COTTON, R.F.A. 8th Battery R.F.A. is attached.	Appendix 247.
	✗ This again emphasises the inadvisability of individual units being detailed specially by higher authority, when a unit is required for a special task. Obviously the C.R.A. is the best judge of which of his Brigades is the batter situated to perform certain work, and also which he can best spare. See also Appendix 239, also remarks June 5th and June 6th.	

(9 29 6) W 4141—463 100,000 9/14 HWV

Army Form C. 2118.

WAR DIARY
or
INTELLIGENCE SUMMARY.
(*Erase heading not required.*)

Instructions regarding War Diaries and Intelligence Summaries are contained in F. S. Regs., Part II. and the Staff Manual respectively. Title pages will be prepared in manuscript.

Hour, Date, Place	Summary of Events and Information	Remarks and references to Appendices
12.55.a.m. 9th June 1915.	14th Battery fired at Bomb Gun W. of P.14 at request of Infantry.	
LA CROIX MARMEUSE.		
8.45.a.m. do.	15.c.m. howitzer shelled vicinity S 20 c.	
9.45.a.m. do.	8th Battery fired on Germans working in the open 100 yards S.W. of P.12.	
10.5.a.m. to 11.a.m. do.	66th Battery fired at intervals on German trenches in retaliation to PIPSQUEAKS shelling our support trenches.	
10.30.a.m. and } do. 4.p.m. }	8th Battery retaliated on R.8. to Q.18.	
11.20.a.m. do.	8th Battery retaliated on enemys trenches for shelling our front line behind V.2. and our support trench behind V.1.	+ Appendix 13+
11.25.a.m, 11.42.a.m. do. 11.45.a.m., 3.40.p.m. } 4.15.p.m., 4.20.p.m., } do. and 4.27.p.m. }	2nd Battery retaliated on enemy's front trenches for shelling ours	
11.45.p.m. do.	14th Battery fired a few rounds on working party near Q.8.	
11.45.a.m. and 3.40.p.m. do.	PIPSQUEAK active on our trenches.	
12.10.p.m. do.	7th Battery fired a few rounds on German trenches.	
1.50.p.m. do.	PIPSQUEAK fired a few rounds on road in front of 14th Battery position (S 2 c).	
3.20.p.m. do.	PIPSQUEAK fired at junction of road S. of RICHEBOURG.	
3.30.p.m. do.	Enemy shelled house at S 5 c 5'4 with 21.c.m. howitzer-getting 3 direct hits.	
	15.c.m. howitzer shelled N.W. of RICHEBOURG and in the region of the RITZ.	
4.p.m. do.	PIPSQUEAK shelled support trenches near LEICESTER LOUNGE vigorously.	
4.3.p.m. do.	Light howitzer shelled RICHEBOURG (Some reports say 21.c.m.)	
4.30.p.m. do.	8th Battery fired a few rounds on V.3. to R.8. and at ruined cottage near Q.12.	
8.30.p.m. do.	8th Battery shelled enemy's trenches for a quarter of an hour in reply to hostile shelling of support trenches of GARHWAL Brigade by PIPSQUEAKS.	
	* For further information see Tactical Progress Report attached.	* Appendix 27+

Army Form C. 2118.

WAR DIARY
or
INTELLIGENCE SUMMARY.
(Erase heading not required.)

Instructions regarding War Diaries and Intelligence Summaries are contained in F.S. Regs., Part II. and the Staff Manual respectively. Title pages will be prepared in manuscript.

Hour, Date, Place	Summary of Events and Information	Remarks and references to Appendices
9.5.a.m.,10.35.a.m.) 10th June and 4.45.p.m.) 1915... LA CROIX MARMEUSE.	66th Battery retaliated on enemy trenches.	
12 noon. do......	10.5.c.m. Howitzers shelled LA COUTURE for about two hours, firing one round every ten minutes.	
3.p.m. do......	Same battery(probably) shelled KING' Road(X 11), true bearing of report 104° from X 18 a. 4˙5.	
5.15.p.m.to 7.p.m. do......	Same battery(probably) switched down to LE TOURET- firing at intervals.	
8.1.p.m. do......	MEERUT Division No.G-324 * received regarding the section of the 55th Howitzer Battery to be placed at the disposal of the LAHORE Division. This section which was temporarily detached from the 8th Division has just completed registration of points and objectives on the front of the MEERUT Division.	* Appendix 249.
	=	
	PIPSQUEAK shelled vicinity of RUE du BOIS, LA COUTURE, VEILLE CHAPELLE and PONT du HEM with a few rounds during the day. Two light shell fell in the neighbourhood of Chateau at LA CROIX MARMEUSE during the afternoon- one was blind.	
	Report on the work done by the 1st and 4th Brigades R.G.A. who are operating on the MEERUT Division front is given in the Tactical Progress Report attached. %	% Appendix 250.
	G.O.C., R.A., MEERUT Division No.750-R.A.(L) on his experiences and opinions on various points connected with operations of the present war, called for by the Brigadier General, R.A., Indian Corps is attached.	% Appendix 251.

Army Form C. 2118.

WAR DIARY
or
INTELLIGENCE SUMMARY.
(Erase heading not required.)

Instructions regarding War Diaries and Intelligence Summaries are contained in F.S. Regs., Part II. and the Staff Manual respectively. Title pages will be prepared in manuscript.

Hour, Date, Place	Summary of Events and Information	Remarks and references to Appendices
8th June 1915. LA CROIX MARMEUSE.		*Appendix 154*
4.a.m. to 5.a.m.	Observation of fire very difficult to-day owing to mist.	
9.20.a.m.	10.5.c.m. howitzer shelled trenches of BAREILLY Brigade. PIPSQUEAK shelled front trenches from direction of LORGIES, and a few crumps were put in near RITZ from direction of BOIS du BIEZ.	
10.30.a.m.	PIPSQUEAK and WOOLY BEARS(10.5.c.m. howitzer)shelled trenches in vicinity P.4.- P.5 from direction of VIOLAINES.	
About 12 noon.	German 105 mm howitzer shelled various parts of our trenches.	
12.30.p.m.	8th Battery fired into a tree near R.10, suspected as snipers or observation post- the branches apparently being arranged for such purpose.	
1.p.m. to 3.p.m.	PIPSQUEAK shelled communication trench to V.1. and fire trench at intervals.	
2.15.p.m.	WOOLY Bears shelled Indian Village (S 20 b.d.).	
3.p.m.	2nd Battery fired a few rounds at a german working party seen near R.8. This was repeated at 4.p.m.	
About 3.p.m.	PIPSQUEAKS retaliated several times in a lively manner whilst 8th Battery were registering V.3.	
3.30.p.m.	2nd Battery fired a few rounds at a german working party seen near R.8.	
3.30.p.m. to 4.15.p.m.	10.5.c.m. howitzer shelled M.27.d.	
4.p.m.	PIPSQUEAK put a few shells into LA COUTURE.	
4.15.p.m.	10.5.c.m. howitzer shelled 19th Battery(S 7 b 1'6) for 20 minutes. 10.5.c.m. howitzer from direction of LORGIES- appeared very close- shelled LA COUTURE also KING's Road.	
4.20.p.m.	PIPSQUEAK shelled INDIAN VILLAGE.	
4.30.p.m.	2nd Battery fired on Germans crossing fields beyond Q.16.	
5.10.p.m.	WOOLY BEARS shelled INDIAN VILLAGE fairly heavily for about 40 mins. Same battery switched on to Reserve trenches S 15 c for about 15 minutes.	
	For further information see Tactical Progress Report attached.	*Appendix 252.

Army Form C. 2118.

WAR DIARY
or
INTELLIGENCE SUMMARY.
(Erase heading not required.)

Instructions regarding War Diaries and Intelligence Summaries are contained in F. S. Regs., Part II. and the Staff Manual respectively. Title pages will be prepared in manuscript.

Hour, Date, Place	Summary of Events and Information	Remarks and references to Appendices
=12th June 1915..... LA CROIX MARMEUSE.		
7.50.a.m.	During the morning 15.c.m. howitzer shelled our support trenches in vicinity of P.1. intermittently, and PIPSQUEAK did the same about M.9. PIPSQUEAKS fired on our trenches intermittently all day— about 50% of the shell were blind.	
8.30.a.m.	15.c.m. howitzer shelled INDIAN VILLAGE(S 20 a).	
8.35.a.m.	WOOLY BEARS shelled the vicinity of S 19 b(6 rounds).	
do........	66th Battery fired a few rounds at enemy's trenches in retaliation to enemy shelling ours.	
9.10.a.m.	PIPSQUEAK shelled 14th Battery O.P.(14 b 8'7 1/10,000 map).	
9.30.a.m.	10.5.c.m. howitzer fired on our trenches near R.3.	
9.45 to 10.a.m.	15.c.m. howitzer shelled vicinity S 14 a(a field just N. of RUE du BOIS) nearly all were blind owing to soft ground, but detonated well on the road.	
11.15.a.m.	8th Battery fired in retaliation.	
11.30.a.m.	15.c.m. howitzer shelled support trenches at N.12— 4 rounds battery fire one second— intervals good— range too short.	
12.35.p.m.	14th Battery fired on trench 100 yards S.W. of P.14. Explosion in trench one second after shell burst. Likely bombs exploding.	Appendix 15
12.45.p.m.	8th Battery registered points near DOLL'S HOUSE.	
12.57.p.m., and 3.30.p.m.	2nd Battery fired at probable O.P. in tree near Q.15.	
5.30.p.m.		
1.45.p.m.	15.c.m. howitzer fired on our communication trench near FACTORY causing some casualties.	
2.p.m.	15.c.m. howitzer fired on EDWARD Road.	
2.55.p.m.	2nd Battery fired in retaliation.	
3.p.m.	15.c.m. howitzer shelled our trenches in rear of V.2. from direction of LORGIES.	
3.15.p.m.	Two 15.c.m. howitzer shell fell near 14th Battery position—one blind.	
4.p.m.	PIPSQUEAK shelled 19th Battery position(S 7 b 1'8). 66th Battery fired a few rounds at house near P.16 where three Huns were seen to enter.	
4.30.p.m.	8th Battery fired salvos in conjunction with MOTHER, who was ranging on communication trenches S.E. of QUINQUE RUE. 44th Battery fired a few rounds on communication trenches S.E. of P.18 and registered a point on QUINQUE RUE.	DOLL'S HOUSE S23 & 9.8
4.45.p.m.	8th Battery fired a few rounds at tree near R.13—supposed O.P..	

Army Form C. 2118.

WAR DIARY
or
INTELLIGENCE SUMMARY.
(Erase heading not required.)

Instructions regarding War Diaries and Intelligence Summaries are contained in F. S. Regs., Part II. and the Staff Manual respectively. Title pages will be prepared in manuscript.

Hour, Date, Place	Summary of Events and Information	Remarks and references to Appendices
4.50.p.m. 12th June 1915. LA CROIX MARMEUSE.	PIPSQUEAK shelled our Reserve trenches in front of INDIAN VILLAGE from direction of LORGIES. PIPSQUEAK was again active at 5.15.p.m.	x Appendix 154
5.30.p.m. do......	PIPSQUEAK shelled vicinity of X 18 b.	
5.35.p.m. do......	2nd Battery registered on ridge S.W. of Q.15.	
6.10.p.m. do......	2nd Battery fired at german waving flag in trench in S. part of FERME du BOIS.	
	The work done by the 1st and 4th Brigades R.G.A. operating on the MEERUT Division front is shown in the Tactical Progress Report which is attached.	*Appendix 253.

Army Form C. 2118.

WAR DIARY
or
INTELLIGENCE SUMMARY.
(Erase heading not required.)

Instructions regarding War Diaries and Intelligence Summaries are contained in F.S. Regs., Part II. and the Staff Manual respectively. Title pages will be prepared in manuscript.

Hour, Date, Place	Summary of Events and Information	Remarks and references to Appendices
6.50.a.m. 13th June 1915. LA CROIX MARMEUSE.	66th Battery fired at trenches near Q.12 in reply to Huns shelling our reserve trenches.	
8.30.a.m. do.	Heavy howitzer shelled position lately vacated by 7th Battery just S. of RICHEBOURG. 15.c.m. howitzer shelled INDIAN VILLAGE (S 20 b.d.).	
8.45.a.m. do.	8th Battery fired a few rounds at Germans seen working near Q.15.	
9.15.a.m. do.	WOOLY BEARS shelled vicinity of INDIAN VILLAGE, from direction just N. of LA BASSEE.	
10.5.a.m. do.	Heavy howitzer shelled old and reserve trenches S.E. of RUE du BOIS.	x Appendix 154
10.a.m. do.	15.c.m. howitzer shelled vicinity of Q.7.	New Tran down from
10.30.a.m. do.	Heavy howitzer shelled PRINCES Road, thought to be registering KING'S Road to DEAD COW FARM, aeroplane to S.E. seen to be observing for this battery.	
10.30.a.m. do.	8th Battery fired registering rounds at Q.8 and Q.9.	
10.35.a.m. do.	15.c.m. howitzer shelled X Road RUE de l'EPINETTE-RUE du BOIS.	
11.30.a.m. do.	2nd Battery fired a few rounds on Q.15 to check registration.	
12.15.p.m. do.	15.c.m. howitzer shelled BREWERY (S 20 c) for half an hour.	
12.25.p.m. do.	15.c.m.(10.5.c.m ?)howitzer shelled vicinity X 18 c for over and hour at odd intervals.	
3.40.p.m. do.	44th Battery fired on FERME COUR d'AVOINE in retaliation.	
3.45.p.m. do.	WOOLY Bears shelled RUE de l'EPINETTE ( ) at 3.45.p.m. Joined by PIPSQUEAKS at 4.p.m. firing salvos and later at 4.30.p.m. 15.c.m.	
4.p.m. and 4.30.p.m.	howitzer at X road X 18 c and vicinity until 5.15.p.m.	
4.p.m. do.	14th Battery fired on M.12 and M.14 in retaliation to PIPSQUEAKS firing on our trenches.	
4.45.p.m. do.	WOOLY BEARS shelled track from INDIAN VILLAGE to RUE de l'EPINETTE.	
6.20.p.m. do.	15.c.m. howitzer and PIPSQUEAK shelled vicinity of RUE des BERCEAUX.	
6.30.p.m. to 7.15.p.m do.	Area X 17 and X 18 and vicinity bombarded by PIPSQUEAK and 10.5.c.m. howitzer in retaliation to shelling of enemy's wire by HIGHLAND Divisional Artillery.	
	Work carried out by the 4th Brigade R.G.A. operating on the MEERUT Division front will be seen in the Tactical Progress Report attached.	*Appendix 254.

Army Form C. 2118.

WAR DIARY
or
INTELLIGENCE SUMMARY.
(Erase heading not required.)

Instructions regarding War Diaries and Intelligence Summaries are contained in F.S. Regs., Part II. and the Staff Manual respectively. Title pages will be prepared in manuscript.

Hour, Date, Place	Summary of Events and Information	Remarks and references to Appendices
14th June 1915. LA CROIX MARMEUSE.	German guns very quiet during the whole day.	
4.15.a.m.	2nd Battery fired on German working party seen digging at Q.16. The Party made off, but re-appeared and was again fired at at 5.15.a.m. — it then stopped work.	
7.45.a.m.	15.c.m. howitzer shelled RUE de l'EPINETTE.	
8.a.m.	44th Battery shelled position near M.14 where PIPSQUEAK flashes were seen.	
9.15.a.m.	44th Battery fired 10 rounds at O.P. near Q.15 at request of Infantry.	
9.25.a.m.	Enemy howitzer (probably 15 .c.m.) shelled 7th Battery O.P. orchard (S 21 a.) from direction of LA BASSEE.	
	15.c.m. howitzer shelled support trenches and communication trench in front of Indian Village (S 20 b.d.) from direction of LORGIES.	Appendix 154
9.50.a.m.	WOOLY BEARS shelled vicinity of S 13 b.	
12 noon.	PIPSQUEAK active on our front trenches and communication trench near V.1.	
	8th Battery registered trench Q.17 to P.19 with view to co-operation with 4th Corps.	
1.p.m. to 2.p.m.	10.5.c.m. howitzer shelled REVOLVER HOUSE (S 3 a) and S 2 d.	
1.30.p.m.	Light howitzer and PIPSQUEAK shelled road between WINDY CORNER and St VAAST.	
2.30.p.m.	WOOLY BEARS shelled track from INDIAN VILLAGE to RUE de l'EPINETTE for half an hour.	
2.50.p.m.	2nd Battery registered P.18 and Q.12 with view to co-operation with 4th Corps.	
	14th Battery fired a few rounds at intervals in retaliation for germans shelling our trenches.	
5.50.p.m.	66th Battery fired 4 rounds at enemy's working party S.E. of L.17 — fire effective.	
	Work carried out by the 4th Brigade R.G.A. operating on the MEERUT Division front is given in the attached Tactical Progress Report*.	*Appendix 255.
	Orders issued for the batteries of the 13th Brigade R.F.A. to co-operate with the 4th Corps vide Appendices 256, 257, 258, 259, 260, 261, 262, 263 and 264.	Appendices 256 to 264.

Army Form C. 2118.

WAR DIARY
or
INTELLIGENCE SUMMARY.
(Erase heading not required.)

Instructions regarding War Diaries and Intelligence Summaries are contained in F.S. Regs, Part II. and the Staff Manual respectively. Title pages will be prepared in manuscript.

Hour, Date, Place	Summary of Events and Information	Remarks and references to Appendices
7.45.p.m. 14th June 1915 to 4.30.a.m. 15th June 1915 LA CROIX MARMEUSE.	2nd and 8th Batteries carried out Barrages as ordered, to co-operate with IV Corps i.e., P.19 to Q.17 and P.18 to Q.13, a few rounds every half hour.	
11.15.a.m. 15th June 1915.... LA CROIX MARMEUSE.	During the night 14th/15th June 66th Battery fired a few rounds on enemy's working party near Q.11 at request from Infantry. PIPSQUEAKS shelled our support trenches.	
11.20.a.m. do......	2nd Battery engaged DISTILLERY as ordered by MEERUT Division, on information from INDIAN Corps that several motor cars were halted in road outside. Probably Staff observing from there.	Appendix 13 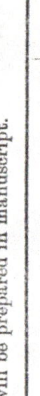
11.45.a.m. do......	14th and 66th Batteries fired a few rounds at German trenches in retaliation to their shelling ours.	
12.30.p.m. do......	14th Battery fired at working party W. of P.14 at request of Infantry.	
1.20.p.m. do......	Heavy howitzer shelled fire trench of "A" Sub-section.	
3.20.p.m. do......	66th Battery shelled sand-bagged house S. of Q.12 in retaliation to Germans shelling our trenches N. of Q.7.	
3.35.p.m.to 4.p.m. do......	15.c.m. howitzer and PIPSQUEAK shelled CROIX BARBEE and to N.W. of that point. About 50 shell. Ten casualties near Cross Roads.	
5.45.p.m.to 8.45.p.m.do......	P.19 to Q.17 and P.18 to Q.12 were barraged at slow rate to assist operations of 4th Corps.	
6.p.m. do......	8th Battery fired a few rounds in retaliation to germans firing on trenches of "B" Sub-section.	
6.p.m. to 7.p.m. do......	15.c.m. and 10.5.c.m. howitzers shelled RUE du BOIS and RUE des BERCEAUX.	
9.20.p.m. do......	Two heavy "crumps" fell in front of 14th Battery position in S 2 c.	
	During the afternoon enemy shelled road N. of WINDY CORNER.	
	The work done by the 4th Brigade R.G.A. is shown in the daily Tactical Progress Report*.	* Appendix 265.

Army Form C. 2118.

WAR DIARY
or
INTELLIGENCE SUMMARY.
(Erase heading not required.)

Instructions regarding War Diaries and Intelligence Summaries are contained in F.S. Regs., Part II. and the Staff Manual respectively. Title pages will be prepared in manuscript.

Hour, Date, Place	Summary of Events and Information	Remarks and references to Appendices
16th June 1915. LA CROIX MARMEUSE.	2nd and 8th Batteries carried out firing during the night 15th/16th and today as order (Barrages P.18 to Q.12 and P.19 to Q.17) to co-operate with IV Corps.	
8.45.p.m.) to 15th June 1915. 11.15.p.m.)	Heavy howitzer (21.c.m.) shelled a little short of 14th Battery from direction of ILLIES.	
10.40.a.m. 16th June 1915. LA CROIX MARMEUSE.	15.c.m. howitzer shelled trenches near P.8. till 11.20.a.m. from direction of LORGIES. Again active at 3.30.p.m.	
11.a.m. do	44th Battery fired at PIPSQUEAK whose flashes were observed in direction of M.25 fired up to 6,100 yards but failed to reach it.	x Appendix 265a
11.40.a.m. do	PIPSQUEAK at M.30 active.	x Appendix 154
2.20.p.m. do	Orders received from Indian Corps for one 18 pr. Battery to be placed at disposal of 9th Brigade R.F.A. for co-operation with IV Corps. 7th Battery was selected for this and task allotted.	
2.35.p.m. do	66th Battery fired at trenches S. of P.17 in retaliation for shelling of our reserve trenches by heavy howitzers.	
3.18.p.m. do	14th Battery fired a few rounds a trenches in retaliation. 7th Battery fired at germ trench L.12 to 200 yards E.N.E. till 5.30 p.m. to co-operate with IV Corps (see 2.20.p.m.m)	
4.30.p.m. do	2nd and 8th Batteries again formed barrages at slow rate until 7.30. p.m. to co-operate with IV Corps.	d Appendix 265
4.50.p.m. do	14th Battery fired at O.P. M.12 in response to PIPSQUEAK shelling trenches.	*Appendix 266.
6.p.m. do	66th Battery fired on sand-bagged house S.E. of P.15 in retaliation for PIPSQUEAK firing on our reserve trenches	
	Observed Barrage OG 478 received re 4th Corps recommence operations.	
	For further information see Tactical Progress Report attached.	

Army Form C. 2118.

WAR DIARY
or
INTELLIGENCE SUMMARY.
(Erase heading not required.)

Instructions regarding War Diaries and Intelligence Summaries are contained in F.S. Regs., Part II. and the Staff Manual respectively. Title pages will be prepared in manuscript.

Hour, Date, Place	Summary of Events and Information	Remarks and references to Appendices
17th June 1915. LA CROIX MARMEUSE.	Batteries of the 4th Brigade R.F.A. fired a few rounds in retaliation to germans shelling our trenches.	
7.50.a.m.	PIPSQUEAK fired a few rounds at our communication trenches during the morning.	
9.20.a.m.	WOOLY BEARS shelled vicinity S.W. of BREWERY(S 20 c) from direction of VIOLAINES.	
Between 10.a.m. and 11.a.m.	15.c.m. howitzer shelled vicinity of S 19 c. Some 10.5.c.m. and PIPSQUEAK fell near CROIX BARBEE.	
11.a.m. to 12 noon.do.	10.5.c.m. howitzer fired on CROIX BARBEE direction, and also on line through recent position of 44th Battery towards the 48th Heavy Battery.	x Appendix 154
11.5.a.m.	15.c.m. howitzer and PIPSQUEAK shelled support trenches in front of INDIAN VILLAGE.	
11.30.a.m.	Six 10.5.c.m. shell fell within near position lately occupied by 44th Battery.	
11.50.a.m.	One shell fell within four yards of Headquarters of 4th Brigade R.F.A. wounding two gunners.	
12.30.p.m.	8th Battery registered new line of trench marked out with stakes between FERME du BOIS and R.9. x	
3.p.m.	15.c.m. howitzer shelled house S 25 b 5'7(3 direct hits) and reserve trenches in front of INDIAN VILLAGE.	
3.30.p.m.	21.c.m. howitzer shelled reserve trenches in front of FESTUBERT, also front line trench near QUINQUE RUE.	
4.15.p.m.	14th Battery fired a few rounds in conjunction with 48th Heavy Battery shelling P.14. x 48th Heavy Battery scored several direct hits on ruin of which only portions of walls existed before.	My 9
6.p.m.	10.5.c.m. howitzer fired towards DOLL's House M 27 d 7'4.	
	For further information see Tactical Progress Report attached.	* Appendix 267.

Army Form C. 2118.

WAR DIARY
or
INTELLIGENCE SUMMARY.
(Erase heading not required.)

Instructions regarding War Diaries and Intelligence Summaries are contained in F.S. Regs., Part II. and the Staff Manual respectively. Title pages will be prepared in manuscript.

Hour, Date, Place	Summary of Events and Information	Remarks and references to Appendices
18th June 1915. LA CROIX MARMEUSE.	77.mm. shelled communication trenches of Highland Division a good deal during the night, and Reserve trenches S. of INDIAN VILLAGE.	*Appendices 267 a + b
4.40.a.m. do.........	Very little hostile field gun shelling to-day.	
7.15.a.m. do.........	77.mm. shelled trenches round M.9. very heavily.	
	2nd Battery fired 6 rounds on DISTILLERY owing to german field guns shelling RUE du BOIS.	
7.42.a.m. do.........	14th Battery fired at M.12.- registration for IV Corps operations.	9.30.a.m.
8.30.a.m. do.........	15.c.m. howitzer shelled support trenches L.5 - L.7.	Report received C.527
8.50.a.m. do.........	66th Battery fired at sand-bagged house S.E. of P.17. in conjunction with 48th Heavy Battery, which obtained 3 direct hits.	received re operations of 4th Corps - postponed for 24 hours - commencement
11.a.m. do.........	8th Battery fired at germans working in their trench between R.8. and Q.15.	8 a.m. + 13th Div R.F.A.
11.a.m. to 12 noon.do.........	Heavy howitzers fired short of 41th Heavy Battery dropping shells about M 31 b.	*Appendix 154
11.30.a.m. do.........	44th Battery fired 12 rounds at a farm near P.18.	
11.45.a.m. do.........	14th Battery registered X.14, X.18, X.19, and X.20 - task for co-operation with IV Corps.	
12.noon. do.........	15.c.m. howitzer shelled FESTUBERT.	
1.20.p.m. do.........	15.c.m. howitzer shelled vicinity X 18 c, S.13.b for an hour in bursts of 2 and 4 rounds.	
1.30.p.m. to 2.30.p.m. do...	Heavy howitzers fired on area S.W. of RICHEBOURG(believed to be 21.c.m.).	
1.47.p.m. do.........	66th Battery fired at sandbagged house S.E. of P.17. in reply to enemy shelling our trenches.	
1.50.p.m. do.........	Leicester's trenches were heavily shelled by heavy howitzers- 2nd Battery retaliated on the DISTILLERY getting some nice hits; but this did not stop fire of heavy howitzers.	
3.10.p.m. do.........	2nd Battery registered points for co-operation with IV Corps.	
4.30.p.m. and) do.........	8th Battery fired on working party in trench near R.10.	
5.25.p.m.)		
5.10.p.m. to 7.10.p.m. do...	21.c.m. howitzer believed to be at WARNETON(T10 c 2'2)was firing on RUE des BERCEAUX with wireless aeroplane observation. Aeroplane gave 2 "Targets" and "O.K." on old Highland Artillery position before flying home last time.	
6.15.p.m. do.........	14th Battery fired at working party 70 yards S.W. of P.14.	
7.45.p.m. do.........	Section 55th Howitzer Battery registered Q.15 and P.14.	
	Daily Tactical Progress Report* attached.	Appendix 268.

* Appendix

Army Form C. 2118.

WAR DIARY
or
INTELLIGENCE SUMMARY.
(Erase heading not required.)

Instructions regarding War Diaries and Intelligence Summaries are contained in F. S. Regs., Part II. and the Staff Manual respectively. Title pages will be prepared in manuscript.

Hour, Date, Place	Summary of Events and Information	Remarks and references to Appendices
3.30.a.m. to)19th June 1915. 4.a.m.) LA CROIX MARMEUSE.	3.30.a.m. to 3.40.a.m. 14th Battery bombarded trench X.16 to Z.3.with H.E. and shrapnel. At 3.43.a.m. to E.53.a.m. searched 300 yards with shrapnel. At 3.53.a.m. to 4.a.m. resumed on trench with H.E. and shrapnel. Co-operation with IV Corps demonstration.	※ Appendix 268a
3.45.a.m. do.........	Guns at M.30. reported active, also some new flashes located 100 yards from M.30, N.E. along road.	
7.15.a.m. do.........	15.c.m. howitzer shelled vicinity L.8. in retaliation to the 3.30.a.m. bombardment of hostile trenches by IV Corps. 66th Battery fired on sand-bagged house in retaliation for 77.mm. firing on our trenches. At three other times during the day same battery fired at same house in retaliation to germans firing on our trenches.	
7.45.a.m. do.........	77.mm. gun shelled vicinity X 23 d for about $\frac{1}{2}$ hour. 15.c.m. howitzer shelled vicinity S 20 d for $\frac{1}{2}$ hour and M.5. for 15 minutes.	
10.5.a.m. do.........	Heavy howitzer shelled PRINCES Road, probable direction LORGIES.	
11.30.a.m. do.........	15x50xxxx 10.5.c.m. howitzer shelled vicinity S 20 c 9'1 for over half an hour (BREWERY).	
12 noon. do.........	14th Battery fired in retaliation on trenches S.W. of P.14.	
1.p.m. do.........	Some 77.m.m. shell fired on trenches in front of "SAVOY"(S 9 c 5'0). Road in S 20 b shelled by howitzer- direction ILLIES.	
2.30.p.m. do.........	15.c.m. howitzer shelled vicinity of DEAD COW FARM and communication trench near N.6.	
2.37.p.m. do.........	Howitzer active on trenches of "A" Sub-section-supposed direction of LORGIES.	
3.25.p.m. do.........	Howitzer shells were dropping in front of 14th Battery from direction of LORGIES.	
3.30.p.m. do.........	Section of 55th Howitzer Battery registered P.14 and Q.15.	
4.p.m. do.........	Two heavy howitzer shell fell short of 48th Heavy Battery.	
5.15.p.m. do.........	8th Battery fired shrapnel and H.E. and new barriade half way between R.11 and R.11 13.	
6.15.p.m. do.........	7th Battery fired a few rounds to register the night lines, having returned to MEERUT Division control from IV Corps.	

Army Form C. 2118.

WAR DIARY
or
INTELLIGENCE SUMMARY.
(Erase heading not required.)

Instructions regarding War Diaries and Intelligence Summaries are contained in F. S. Regs., Part II. and the Staff Manual respectively. Title pages will be prepared in manuscript.

Hour, Date, Place	Summary of Events and Information	Remarks and references to Appendices
6.55.p.m. 19th June 1915. LA CROIX BARBEE.	2nd Battery registered barricade in course of construction on LA QUINQUE RUE; obtaining 3 hits. For further information see Tactical Progress Report attached.	*Appendix 269.

Army Form C. 2118.

WAR DIARY
or
INTELLIGENCE SUMMARY.
(Erase heading not required.)

Hour, Date, Place	Summary of Events and Information	Remarks and references to Appendices
5.30.a.m. 20th June 1915. LA CROIX MARMEUSE.	14th Battery fired at M.12 and P.14 in retaliation for 77.mm. shell-ing our trenches.	
9.30.a.m. do.	Light howitzer shelled along the RUE du BOIS.	
9.55.a.m. do.	Heavy howitzer shelled the breastwork in rear of the "SAVOY". 66th Battery fired at sand-bagged house S. of P.17 in reply to howitzer firing on our trenches. (*Appendix* O.P.)	
10.a.m. do.	2 shell fell in vicinity of M 31 b.	
11.a.m. to 11.20.a.m do.	21.c.m. howitzer shelled vicinity of house 200 yards N. of M.7.	
12 noon. do.	8th Battery fired 5 rounds at barricade half way between R.11 and R.13.	× Appendix 154
1.30.p.m. do.	14th Battery fired at M.20 - a gun was firing from near this point.	
2.30.p.m. and) do.	10.5.c.m. howitzer shelled the BREWERY(S 20 c 10'3).	
3.15.p.m.)	7th Battery fired a few rounds at houses near P.14 at request of Infantry, who reported snipers in that direction.	
2.45.p.m. do.	14th Battery fired at P.14 to stop sniping.	
3.p.m. do.	10.5.c.m. howitzer shelled vicinity of REVOLVER HOUSE(S 3 c 5'4).	
3.30.p.m. do.	77.mmm. shelled along the RUE du BOIS.	
4.45.p.m. do.	14th Battery registered house on right of M.23. 77.mm. thought to be firing from near there on St VAAST-RITZ Road; gun stopped at once.	
5.30.p.m. do.	2nd Battery fired at hostile working party behind FERME du BOIS.	
5.45.p.m. and) do.	8th Battery fired at German working party at Q.16.	
6.15.p.m.)		
	During the afternoon 10.5.c.m. howitzer and 77.mm. guns shelled the trenches intermittently, also 21.c.m. howitzer shelled FESTUBERT.	* Appendix 270.
	Orders received from MEERUT Division that the 9th Brigade R.F.A. would rejoin the MEERUT Division from its present work in co-operation with IV Corps.	∅ Appendix 271
	For further information see Tactical Progress Report.	

Army Form C. 2118.

WAR DIARY
or
INTELLIGENCE SUMMARY.
(Erase heading not required.)

Hour, Date, Place	Summary of Events and Information	Remarks and references to Appendices
21st June 1915. LA CROIX MARMEUSE.	Enemy's Artillery very much more active to-day than it has been for many days.	
	During night 20th/21st Salvoes of 6 rounds were fired at odd intervals at communication trench in front of "Savoy".	
5.15.a.m. do.	66th Battery fired at sand-bagged house S. of P.17 in retaliation to 77.mm firing on our trenches. 77.mm. stopped firing. (Sketch 8.?)	Appendix 154
6.a.m. do.	77.mm. active on left of "D" Sub-section trenches. 8th Battery fired a few rounds at germans working at white sand-bag trench in Orchard of FERME du BOIS. Repeated at 4.30.p.m. using a few H.E.	
8.a.m. to 9.30.a.m. do.	15.c.m. howitzer shelled road M.27.d. and road running N.W. Two houses were set on fire.	
9.a.m. do.	Heavy howitzers shelled vicinity of ROUGE CROIX.	
Between 9 and 10.a.m. do.	10.5.c.m. howitzer shelled vicinity of PRINCES Road.	
9.50.a.m. and } 12 noon. } do.	German heavy howitzer (21.c.m.) shelled QUEEN MARY Road-real object appeared to be corner house S 2 c 3'3 on which a direct hit was obtained.	
12 noon. do.	10.5.c.m. howitzer shelled vicinity of WINDY CORNER.	
12.30.p.m. do.	14th Battery fired at M.12 and M.14 in retaliation for 77.mm. firing on WINDY CORNER- 77.mm. stopped firing.	
	About 12 heavy howitzer shell fell at road junction N. of SCHOOL House RICHEBOURG.	
12.45.p.m. do.	Howitzers shelled tramway S 14 d 2'8 from direction of BOIS du BIEZ.	
3.p.m. do.	One 10.5.c.m. shell fell in 19th Battery position.	
3.30.p.m. do.	77.mm. shelled vicinity of S 13 b.	
4.p.m. do.	10.5.c.m. howitzer and 77.mm. gun shelled trenches in front of INDIAN VILLAGE.	
5.9.p.m. do.	*Orders received that 61st Howitzer Battery joining Indian Corps and posted to the MEERUT Division on arrival from BAILLEUL.	* Appendix 272.
5.12.p.m. do.	⌀Orders received that the Section 55th Howitzer Battery would rejoin the 8th Division.	⌀ Appendix 273.
5.45.p.m. do.	7th Battery fired a few rounds near P.14 at request of Infantry-sniping reported from here.	

Army Form C. 2118.

WAR DIARY
or
INTELLIGENCE SUMMARY.
(Erase heading not required.)

Instructions regarding War Diaries and Intelligence Summaries are contained in F. S. Regs., Part II. and the Staff Manual respectively. Title pages will be prepared in manuscript.

Hour, Date, Place	Summary of Events and Information	Remarks and references to Appendices
5.45.p.m. 21st June 1915. to 7.p.m. LA CROIX MARMEUSE.	15.c.m. howitzer shelled assembly trenches S. of CROIX BARBEE and vicinity of Anti Aircraft Gun Section (probably with aeroplane observation).	+ Appendix 154
6.p.m. do	77.mm. shelled our trenches about V.2.	
6.15.p.m. to 6.45.p.m. do	Germans firing salvoes and single rounds of 15.c.m. and 21.c.m. howitzers with aid of aeroplane at house M 32 b 2'2 and vicinity- about 40 rounds fired. Our Anti Aircraft did not open fire.	
8.25.p.m. do	8th Battery fired 24 rounds at Q.15 Redoubt and communication trench which were reported full of men by 1st Brigade R.G.A.	
9.35.p.m. do	77.mm. shelled communication trench in front of "SAVOY".	
	Work done by the 1st and 4th Brigades R.B.A. will be seen in Tactical Progress Report* attached.	* Appendix 274.
6.30.p.m. do	Instructions No.9 of 4th Corps Artillery received and answered (See Appendices 274a and 274b)	Appendices 274a, 274b.
	At the special request of the 4th Corps and with sanction of MEERUT Division the 28th Battery of the 9th Brigade R.F.A. was left with HIGHLAND Divisional Artillery to cover an awkward piece of front round the "ORCHARD" (M.9.), the remaining two batteries returning to MEERUT Division control.	

Army Form C. 2118.

WAR DIARY
or
INTELLIGENCE SUMMARY.
(Erase heading not required.)

Instructions regarding War Diaries and Intelligence Summaries are contained in F.S. Regs., Part II. and the Staff Manual respectively. Title pages will be prepared in manuscript.

Hour, Date, Place	Summary of Events and Information	Remarks and references to Appendices
7.30.a.m. 22nd June 1915. LA CROIX MARMEUSE.	15.c.m. howitzer shelled vicinity X 18 a and S 13 b heavily for over an hour; a burst of 3 and 4 to start with and finishing up with two bursts of 10 rounds each, firing altogether about 100 rounds. Shell scoop from X 18 a 5'5 gave true bearing of 99°.	
7.45.a.m. do	Heavy gun fired on road about S 14 d 7'3 from direction of BOIS du BIEZ.	
8.15.a.m. to 8.45.a.m. do	About 20(15.c.m.)shell fell in vicinity of M 32 a 2'3.	
8.25.a.m. do	Heavy howitzers shelled tram line and first aid post in PRINCES ROAD, also communication trench on right of "A" Sub-section and support trench of left of "A" Sub-section. At least 3 hostile batteries were firing. Aeroplane audible but not visible.	
9.a.m. do	2nd Battery fired 6 rounds at a party of germans behind FERME du BOIS.	*Appendix 154.
9.15.a.m. do	15.c.m. howitzer shelled RICHEBOURG and vicinity- observation by aeroplane over RICHEBOURG.	
9.30.a.m. do	Heavy howitzer shelled South corner of RICHEBOURG.	
10.15.a.m. do	77.mm. shelled 19th Battery position, obtaining a good bracket- no damage. 14th Battery shelled M.23 and behind M.26 in retaliation.	
11.a.m. do	44th Battery registered trench E. of COUR d'AVOUE.	
5.p.m. do	8th Battery fired a few rounds at germans seen in white sand bag trench FERME du BOIS.	
6.20.p.m. do	Shell(?) dropped in field 200 yards W. of 28th Battery position, slightly wounding a French woman working in the field- thought to be a bomb, but may have been german Archie shell; no aeroplane visible or any shelling seen at this time.	
7.10.p.m. do	Hostile howitzer shelled trenches of 3rd LONDON's, in reply to shelling of Q.15 by 8th Siege Battery, they dropped one shell into FERME du BOIS.	
8.50.p.m. do	2nd Battery fired 2 salvoes at Q.15 where enemy were reported in large numbers.	
	During the afternoon the 9th Brigade R.F.A. relieved the 4th Brigade R.F.A. of the Artillery support of the DEHRA DUN Brigade.	*Appendix 275.

For further information see Tactical Progress Report attached:
Forms/C. 2118/10

Army Form C. 2118.

WAR DIARY
or
INTELLIGENCE SUMMARY.
(*Erase heading not required.*)

Instructions regarding War Diaries and Intelligence Summaries are contained in F. S. Regs., Part II. and the Staff Manual respectively. Title pages will be prepared in manuscript.

Hour, Date, Place	Summary of Events and Information	Remarks and references to Appendices
9.30.p.m. 22nd June 1915. LA CROIX MARMEUSE.	Section 55th Howitzer Battery marched out to rejoin 8th Division at PONT du HEM.	
10.p.m. to 11.p.m. do.	3 Batteries of 4th Brigade R.F.A. were withdrawn from action and proceeded into rest billets at St FLORIS.	

Army Form C. 2118

WAR DIARY
or
INTELLIGENCE SUMMARY.
(Erase heading not required.)

Instructions regarding War Diaries and Intelligence Summaries are contained in F.S. Regs, Part II. and the Staff Manual respectively. Title pages will be prepared in manuscript.

Hour, Date, Place	Summary of Events and Information	Remarks and references to Appendices
23rd June 1915. LA CROIX MARMEUSE.	A very quiet day. 8th Battery fired 5 rounds at germans seen working between V.2. and R.8.	
7.30.a.m.	77.mm. gun shelled CHOCOLAT MENIER CORNER from direction of RUE du MARAIS Cross Roads. 61st Howitzer Battery arrived at LA CROIX MARMEUSE from 2nd Army to join MEERUT Division; went into billets for the day. One section was ordered to go into action at S 7 b 1'8 this evening(position lately occupied by Section of 55th Howitzer Battery). Remaining two sections to go into action on 24th. This battery has had a very hard time in the neighbourhood of YPRES.	Appendix 154
4.p.m.	10.5.c.m. howitzer shelled PRINCES ROAD and OLD BRITISH Trench S 15 for half an hour.	Ø Appendix 276
5.p.m.	MEERUT Division Operation Order No.39 received, re MEERUT Division taking over additional portion of line as far North as ORCHARD(S 10 b). Arranged with LAHORE Divisional Artillery that their batteries would cover from V.1. to ORCHARD(inclusive) until MEERUT Batteries could be re-adjusted, vide Appendices 277 and 278.	Appendices 277 and 278
6.15.p.m.	10.5.c.m. howitzer fired on our Reserve trenches from P.3. to about 100 yards W. of L.4.	
7.p.m.	15.c.m. howitzer shelled vicinity of LA COUTURE.	
8.p.m.	Orders received by telephone from Indian Corps that MEERUT Division Artillery must cover front from M.10 to X.16 for night(HIGHLAND Division front). Orders issued by telephone for 19th Battery(9th Brigade R.F.A.) to cover this front, and for one battery of 13th Brigade R.F.A. to cover 19th Battery's normal front(Q.7 to P.19).	* Appendix 279.
	For further information, also work done by 1st and 4th Brigades R.G.A. will be found in Tactical Progress Report attached.	

Army Form C. 2118

WAR DIARY
or
INTELLIGENCE SUMMARY.
(Erase heading not required.)

Instructions regarding War Diaries and Intelligence Summaries are contained in F.S. Regs., Part II. and the Staff Manual respectively. Title pages will be prepared in manuscript.

Hour, Date, Place	Summary of Events and Information	Remarks and references to Appendices
24th June 1915. LA CROIX MARMEUSE.		
10.10.a.m.	Heavy howitzer shell fired at various points throughout the day.	
do	2nd Battery fired a few rounds to make some adjustments in present night lines.	
12 noon.	44th Battery registered on new night lines.	
12.30.p.m.	20th Battery fired a few rounds on enemy's trench opposite P.11 in retaliation for their shelling our front and support trenches at P.10.	
12.30.p.m.	77.mm. fired on our trenches and at other hours of the afternoon.	
1.p.m.	21.c.m.(?) howitzer shelled our support trenches in front of TROCADERO (X18 a 5'8).	
Between 2 & 3.p.m.	15.c.m. howitzer shelled new fire trench W. of FARM CORNER; apparently registering it.	
4.p.m.	2nd Battery fired a few rounds at DISTILLERY to check enemy shelling our trenches.	
4.30.p.m.	8th Battery registered on new night lines Q.16 to Q.11.	
5.5.p.m.	2nd Battery checked registrations in order to be able to take up new night lines when required.	
	Remaining two sections of the 61st Howitzer Battery R.F.A. moved up into action.	
	For further information see Tactical Progress Report attached.	*Appendix 280.
7.45.p.m.	An odd shell, now and then, from a 10.5.c.m. howitzer fell in vicinity of Tram Terminus in KING'S ROAD.	

Army Form C. 2118.

WAR DIARY
or
INTELLIGENCE SUMMARY.
(Erase heading not required.)

Instructions regarding War Diaries and Intelligence Summaries are contained in F. S. Regs., Part II. and the Staff Manual respectively. Title pages will be prepared in manuscript.

Hour, Date, Place	Summary of Events and Information	Remarks and references to Appendices
3.30.p.m. 25th June 1915. LA CROIX MARMEUSE.	44th Battery registered trenches near P.14 for new line.	
5.p.m. do.	15.c.m. howitzer shelled FESTUBERT and 10.5.c.m. howitzer shelled our trenches in vicinity of M.9.	
5.15.p.m. do.	8th Battery registered trench W. of FERME COUR d'AVOUE (new front).	
5.35.p.m. do.	15.c.m. howitzer shelled RUE du BOIS at junction of road at S 15 a.	
6.p.m. do.	Heavy howitzer shelled PRINCES ROAD and CHOCOLAT MENIER CORNER. 2nd Battery checked registration on new front.	
6.30.p.m. do.	.77.mm. shelled between RICHEBOURG and LA COUTURE- mostly blind shell.	
6.45.p.m. do.	10.5.c.m. howitzer shelled vicinity X 17 b.	
	61st Howitzer Battery R.F.A. carried out registration during the day.	
	*	* Appendix 281.
	For further information see Tactical Progress Report attached.	∅ Appendix 281(a). % Appendix 281(b).
	MEERUT Division Operation Order No. 40 received and MEERUT Divisional Artillery No.770-R.A.(L), dated 25th June 1915, issued.	

Army Form C. 2118.

WAR DIARY
or
INTELLIGENCE SUMMARY.

(Erase heading not required.)

Instructions regarding War Diaries and Intelligence Summaries are contained in F.S. Regs., Part II. and the Staff Manual respectively. Title pages will be prepared in manuscript.

Hour, Date, Place	Summary of Events and Information	Remarks and references to Appendices
26th June 1915. LA CROIX MARMEUSE.		
8.30.a.m.	21.c.m. howitzer shelled FESTUBERT continually during the day.	
do.	15.c.m. howitzer shelled vicinity of RUE du BOIS-RUE de l'EPINETTE Cross Roads (a few rounds).	
8.40.a.m.	77.mm. gun shelled our trenches in vicinity of M.9. from direction of VIOLAINES.	x appendix 152
11.a.m.	77.mm. shelled trenches on front of INDIAN VILLAGE for about 20 mins.	
11.30.a.m.	21.c.m. howitzer shelled FESTUBERT- 5 rounds out of 10 were blind.	
11.30.a.m.	44th Battery registered X.31, X.32, to P.14 new frontage.	
11.45.a.m.	77.mm. shelled trenches in front of SAVOY.	
12.15.p.m.	15.c.m. howitzer shelled vicinity of X.18 c (a few rounds).	
1.45.p.m.	10.5.c.m. howitzer shelled vicinity X 17 d for about 20 minutes (a few rounds).	
2.p.m.	10.5.c.m. howitzer shelled REVOLVER HOUSE.	
2.30.p.m.	77.mm. shelled RUE du BOIS.	
4.20.p.m.	77.mm. shelled vicinity X 18 c (a few rounds).	
5.45.p.m.m	2nd Battery fired 50 H.E. on two points near Q.15. These points were indicated by O.C. 2nd and 2nd Gurkhas. The trench in vicinity of these points was repeatedly hit and planks etc., thrown up.	
6.p.m.	Heavy howitzer and 77.mm. shelled our trenches in retaliation for 2nd Battery firing on Q.15. with H.E.	
	During the afternoon the 28th Battery registered N.15 and M.14-4 direct hits on M.14 (an O.P.). Front trench M.9. and M.8. shelled intermittently by 10.5.c.m. howitzer during the afternoon.	* Appendix 282.
	For further information see Tactical Progress Report attached.	

Army Form C. 2118.

WAR DIARY
or
INTELLIGENCE SUMMARY.
(*Erase heading not required.*)

Instructions regarding War Diaries and Intelligence Summaries are contained in F.S. Regs., Part II. and the Staff Manual respectively. Title pages will be prepared in manuscript.

Hour, Date, Place	Summary of Events and Information	Remarks and references to Appendices
8.30.a.m. 27th June 1915. LA CROIX MARMEUSE.	10.5.c.m. howitzer shelled trenches in vicinity of P.7. and P.6.	
9.40.a.m.	15.c.m. howitzer shelled RUE du BOIS-RUE de l'EPINETTE Cross Roads (a few rounds).	
10.45.a.m.	10.5.c.m. howitzer shelled CHOCOLAT MENIER CORNER (about 20 rounds) from direction of LORGIES.	
do.	2nd Battery fired a few rounds at FERME COUR d'AVOUE, where movement was seen.	
12 noon.	Heavy howitzer shelled corner of ALBERT ROAD and RUE du BOIS.	Appendix 1834
12.30.p.m.	15.c.m. howitzer began shelling cross roads S 15 a and then switched to CHOCOLAT MENIER CORNER. O.P. of 20th Battery was knocked down about 60 rounds were fired from direction of VIOLAINES-no casualties.	
1.30.p.m.	44th Battery fired at trench on LA QUINQUE RUE, on suspicion of a bomb gun which had annoyed the 1st 9th Gurkhas.	
4.40.p.m.	15.c.m. howitzer shelled trenches in vicinity of M.9.	
5.p.m.	2nd Battery engaged trenches near Q.15 in retaliation for enemy shelling our fire and support trenches.	
5.p.m.	Three 77.mm. shell fell 150 yards in front of 44th Battery. 77.mm. shelled fire and support trenches in front of SAVOY.	
6.30.p.m.	About 9 heavy howitzer (probably 21.c.m.) fired at RICHEBOURG Church.	
	*	
	For further information see Tactical Progress Report attached.	* Appendix 283.
	∅	∅ Appendix 283(a).
	MEERUT Division Operation Order No.41 received and MEERUT Divisional Artillery No.777-R.A.(L) issued.	% Appendix 283(b).

Army Form C. 2118.

WAR DIARY
or
INTELLIGENCE SUMMARY.
(Erase heading not required.)

Instructions regarding War Diaries and Intelligence Summaries are contained in F.S. Regs., Part II. and the Staff Manual respectively. Title pages will be prepared in manuscript.

Hour, Date, Place	Summary of Events and Information	Remarks and references to Appendices
9.15.a.m. 28th June 1915. LA CROIX MARMEUSE.	44th Battery fired at farm S.E. of P.18 in retaliation for fire on our trenches.	
9.30.a.m.	15.c.m. howitzer shelled vicinity X 24 a 8'3. French Observation ladder in Orchard struck.	
11.a.m.	10.5.c.m. howitzer shelled our trenches in vicinity of M.9.	
11.15.a.m. to 12.15.p.m.	15.c.m. howitzer shelled vicinity of DEAD COW FARM(S 14 d)	
11.30.a.m.	15.c.m. howitzer shelled PRINCES ROAD- hitting house near S 14 d 9'3.	
2.50.p.m.m	21.c.m.(?) howitzer shelled support trenches East of INDIAN VILLAGE. 20th Battery fired some H.E. at houses at M.14 by request of 21st Infantry Brigade.	*Appendix 154.
3.15.p.m.	15.c.m. howitzer again shelled vicinity of DEAD COW FARM.	
3.30.p.m.	15.c.m. howitzer shelled cross roads RUE du BOIS-RUE de l'EPINETTE for about half an hour.	
4.15.p.m.	44th Battery fired 6 rounds at working party carrying planks in trench between P.15 and P.14.	
5.30.p.m.	10.5.c.m. howitzer shelled INDIAN VILLAGE from direction of VIOLAINES.	
6.15.p.m.	77.mm. shelled trenches near R.15 from direction of DISTILLERY.	
6.30.p.m.	44th Battery fired 2 salvoes at supposed field gun position near N.24, the trenches in front of SAVOY having been shelled from that direction.	
	During the afternoon the 20th Battery fired a few rounds at German front trench P.14-N.14. to show points to Battery of the 52nd Brigade taking over from them.	* Appendix 284.
	77.mm. shelled our trenches at various times during the day.	
	For further information see Tactical Progress Report attached.	

Army Form C. 2118.

WAR DIARY
or
INTELLIGENCE SUMMARY.
(Erase heading not required.)

Instructions regarding War Diaries and Intelligence Summaries are contained in F. S. Regs., Part II. and the Staff Manual respectively. Title pages will be prepared in manuscript.

Hour, Date, Place	Summary of Events and Information	Remarks and references to Appendices
10.a.m. 29th June 1915. LA CROIX MARMEUSE.	44th Battery fired one salvo at probable 77.mm. position near N.24.	
11.15.a.m. do.	Two 77.mm. shell burst 300 yards in front of battery just after this. 20th Battery registered FERME de TOULOTTE and fired a few rounds into M.13(a likely O.P.)-two direct hits.	+ Appendix 134
1.10.p.m. do.	44th Battery fired 30 rounds in conjunction with 60 pr. Battery on RUE du MARAIS.	
1.p.m. do.	2nd Battery fired 4 rounds in retaliation for hostile shelling of our trenches.	
1.30.p.m. do.	8th Battery fired at working party in a trench W. of FERME COUR d'AVOUE.	
2.30.p.m. do.	19th Battery fired a few rounds on trenches in vicinity of X.30. in conjunction with Siege Battery firing on that locality.	
5.40.p.m. do.	28th Battery fired 12 rounds on enemy's trenches about X.27 - X.28 in reply to rifle fire on our aeroplane.	
5.45.p.m. do.	Some heavy shell passed over ROUGE CROIX.	
5.55.p.m. do.	Heavy burst of fire on our right probably BIVENCHY for about 5 or 10 minutes. 61st Howitzer Battery registered R.18.	
	A quiet day.	
	For work carried out by the 1st and 4th Brigades R.G.A. see Tactical * Progress Report attached.	* Appendix 285-
	14th and 66th Batteries returned from/St FLORIS and went into action rest at at S 2 c 8.3 and S 7 d 5'6 respectively.	

Army Form C. 2118.

WAR DIARY
or
INTELLIGENCE SUMMARY.
(Erase heading not required.)

Instructions regarding War Diaries and Intelligence Summaries are contained in F.S. Regs., Part II. and the Staff Manual respectively. Title pages will be prepared in manuscript.

Hour, Date, Place	Summary of Events and Information	Remarks and references to Appendices
30th June 1915. LA CROIX MARMEUSE.		× App A5 /54
2.p.m. do........	77.mm. shelled trenches in front of FERME du BOIS and COUR d'AVOUE at irregular intervals during the night 29th/30th. This was being continued at 8.5.a.m. 8th Battery registered new front, relieving a battery of LAHORE Divisional Artillery.	
3.20.p.m.m do.......	Heavy howitzer shelled in direction of 48th Heavy Battery.	
3.55.p.m.m do.......	15.c.m. howitzer shelled vicinity X 24 b (4 rounds).	
4.p.m.m do........	19th Battery registered trenches from FERME du BOIS to V.2. 15.c.m. howitzers shelled INDIAN VILLAGE from direction of VIOLAINES.	
5.45.p.m. do.......	77.mm. shelled neighbourhood of RITZ.	
5.45.p.m. and ⎫ 6.20.p.m.m ⎭ do.......	14th Battery fired 5 rounds on working party between Q.11 and Q.15.	
6.p.m. do.......	44th Battery registered new front relieving a battery of LAHORE Divisional Artillery.	
6.30.p.m.m do.......	15.c.m. howitzer shelled our trenches about S 21 b.	
	* Orders were issued for one section of 17th Battery R.F.A. (St FLORIS) to go into action in relief of one section 28th Battery R.F.A. in X 23 b 8˙5 after dark.	*Appendix 286.
	Instructions for Artillery reliefs taking place to-day were issued.	⌀ Appendix 287.
	For further information, also work done by the 4th Brigade R.G.A. @	@ Appendix 288.
	See Tactical Progress Report attached.	

P.T.O.

Army Form C. 2118.

WAR DIARY
or
INTELLIGENCE SUMMARY.
(Erase heading not required.)

Instructions regarding War Diaries and Intelligence Summaries are contained in F. S. Regs., Part II. and the Staff Manual respectively. Title pages will be prepared in manuscript.

Hour, Date, Place	Summary of Events and Information	Remarks and references to Appendices
30th June 1915....... LA CROIX MARMEUSE.	POSITIONS OF UNITS OF MEERUT DIVISIONAL ARTILLERY ON 30th June 1915. ▼▼▼▼▼▼▼▼▼▼▼▼▼▼▼▼▼▼▼▼▼▼▼▼▼▼▼▼▼▼▼▼▼▼▼ Headquarters MEERUT Divisional Artillery..........R 25 b 0'9. Headquarters 4th Brigade R.F.A............CROIX BARBEE (temporarily) *7th Battery R.F.A.......................At rest(St FLORIS) 14th Battery R.F.A.......................S 2 c 8'3. 66th Battery R.F.A.......................S 7 d 5'6. Headquarters 9th Brigade R.F.A....................X 17 d 8'8 19th Battery R.F.A.............................S 7 b 1'6. 20th Battery R.F.A.............................X 18 a 5'5. ø28th Battery R.F.A............................X 23 b 9'6. Headquarters 13th Brigade R.F.A.................R 29 d 8'8. 2nd Battery R.F.A............................M 32 a 3'7. 8th Battery R.F.A............................M 31 b 9'7. 44th Battery R.F.A...........................M 32 c 10'8. @MEERUT Divisional Ammunition Column............R 26 c 9'9. [signature] Major R.A. Brigade Major, Royal Artillery, MEERUT DIVISION. 1st July 1915.	* One section goes into action in 28th Battery position night 30th June/1st July. ø Under 9th Division pro-tem. One section going out to rest night 30th June/1st July. @ 1 Sect at ZELOBES. 2 sections at PARADIS.

SECRET.

APPENDIX 232

TACTICAL PROGRESS REPORT
1st June 1915.

1(a) ACTION BY OUR OWN ARTILLERY.
7.p.m. 31.5.15. 2nd Battery engaged German working party near V.2.
1st June 1915.
4.0.a.m. 19th Battery from new position registered FERME du BOIS, FERME COUR d'AVOUE and DISTILLERY.
4.30.a.m. 14th Battery registered new trench J.15-K.7, also points K.6 and J.12. Bursts of fire were maintained on this trench throughout the day in accordance with instructions received from the 1st Army.
5.a.m. 28th Battery from new position registered DISTILLERY, Q.8., M.16, M.20., K.12.,P.14., and german front trench opposite P.11 to LA QUINQUE RUE. Two direct hits on P.14.
6.a.m. 66th Battery registered following points with aeroplane:-
S 28 a 4'2- L.17- S 29 c 5'5. 7th Battery registered K.2.-J.12- North and South ends of trench in A 3 b.
9.45.a.m., 3.p.m.,3.25.p.m.)2nd Battery fired on German trenches in
and 3.45.p.m.   )retaliation.
2.20.p.m. 2nd Battery fired on enemy working party near V.2.
3.p.m. 8th Battery registered house Q.11 and Redoubt near Q.15.
3.20.p.m. 2nd Battery engaged PIPSQUEAK Battery located at S.23 c 9'9, which was shelling RICHEBOURG, in co-operation with 48th Heavy Battery-fire was reported as very effective.
5.p.m. 19th Battery registered the following points by aeroplane:-
K.23., M.20., K.12., and trench at centre of S 28.
44th Battery carried our registration during the morning.
66th Battery registered M.15 - M.11.

(b) ACTION BY HOSTILE ARTILLERY.
9.a.m. Neighbourhood of 14th Battery was shelled by PIPSQUEAK for about an hour.
12.25.p.m. PIPSQUEAK shelled trenches between P.10 and Q.7.
3.15.p.m. PIPSQUEAKS were falling 50 yards in rear of 66th Battery in salvoes of three. Appeared to come from LORGIES. This battery was also searching and sweeping country between 66th Battery position and RICHEBOURG. Retort on S 29 a 9'0 claimed to have silenced them, but report from another source located the flashes at S 23 c 9'9.

2. INFORMATION.
MACHINE GUNS:- P.14 is reported to contain a Machine Gun.
HOSTILE BATTERIES:- The two hostile batteries whose flashes were located yesterday(vide Tactical Progress Report 31.5.15) were again firing from same positions to-day. One of these located by flashes in direction of LORGIES true bearing 146° 31' from LANCASTER LOUNGE- Range from battery(by time of report)probably 6,500 yards. This makes battery at S 30 a 5'1, where battery is known to exist.
OBSERVATION POSTS:- M.16 is thought to be a probable O.P.
WIRE ENTANGLEMENTS:- Wire about 2 inches to 2 foot high can be seen in front of road M.20 to L.19.
FIRES:- 5.45.p.m. 14th Battery reported building on E. side of VIOLAINES on fire.
MISCELLANEOUS:- 14th Battery reported that enemy apparently registering their own trenches along points J.15 and J.16.
There appears to be a new trench from about J.12-J.17-not confirmed.
CHANGE of POSITIONS:- 4th Brigade R.F.A. on relief by 18th Brigade R.F.A., and 35th Howitzer Battery R.F.A. moved into new positions last night.

Major R.A.

Brigade Major, Royal Artillery,

Diary 1/6/15 APPENDIX 233

POSITIONS AND ARC'S COVERED BY 9'2" HOWITZERS, 6" GUNS & 60 pr. BATTERIES.

		Position.	Arc.
6" B.L. GUNS	(1) at R 23 b 8'1.		From LA MAISNIL to LA BASSEE.
	(2) at R 29 b 0'0.		From LA MAISNIL to PONT FIX.
3 in number.	(3) at R 35 a 1'9.		From LA MAISNIL to RUE d'OUVERT.
9'2" HOWITZERS	(1) at X 9 c 10'1.		From N 31 d central to A 28 b 9'7.
	(2) at R 36 a 5'6.		From A 21 d 8'8 to T 10 central.
	(3) at R 30 c 3'10.		From A 20 a 1'9 to T.16 central.
4 in number.	(4) at R 30 c 3'10		From A 12 c central to N 28 b cent.

(1) and (2) are for General Bombardment, covering RUE d'OUVERT Railway triangle and CANTELEUX, (3) and (4) are for counter Battery work.

60 Pounders
2 Batteries:-

| 48th Battery. | at R 36 a 4'5 | From S.W. of LA BASSEE to BAS POMMERAU. |
| CANADIAN Battery. | at M 19 d 6'5 | From AUBERS to N. of VIOLAINES. |

APPENDIX 134

"A" Form. Army Form C.2121.

MESSAGES AND SIGNALS.

Prefix SH Code 1-13P Words 35 Charge APPENDIX 234(a) Recd. at 6.58 p.m.
Date 2/6/15
From 7/15
By Lt Bryan B

TO — Meerut D A

Sender's Number: BM 118
Day of Month: 3rd
AAA

Should be glad if your batteries assisting us could fire 10 rds per hour between 6pm and 8pm on their allotted objectives

From / Place: 7th D A
Time: 6.5 PM

SECRET
C.R.A. 57.
O.C. 4th Brigade R.F.A.
  9th Brigade R.F.A.
  1st Brigade R.F.A.

3/6/1915.
APPENDIX 234(?)

1. 1st Division are attacking tonight with the object of capturing enemy's trench from I.4 to I.2 and if possible to extend to point I.9 & H.3.

2. The HIGHLAND Division on our right are making a feint towards RUE du MARAIS.

3. The bombardments will take place as follows:-
   (a) 4 p.m. to 6 p.m. with a cessation of fire from 5 p.m. to 5.15 p.m.
   (b) From 6 p.m. to 9.45 p.m.

4. 4th Brigade R.F.A. are co-operating in this:-
   (i) By firing on communication trench in vicinity L.17.
   (ii) K.13, K.12, K.11 & West
   (iii) L.11, L.12, L.13.

5. Desultory fire will be kept up between 10 p.m. and 3 a.m. by the 4th Brigade Batteries on
   (i) L.17 and approaches
   (ii) K.11, K.12, K.13.

6. HIGHLAND Division will be sending out patrols in neighbourhood of L.17 about 9 p.m.

W. Chrych-Harrison
Major R.A.
Brigade Major R.A.
1st Division.

APPENDIX 235

SECRET.

TACTICAL PROGRESS REPORT
3rd June 1915.

1(a) ACTION BY OUR OWN ARTILLERY.

8.45.a.m. to 11.40.a.m. 2nd Battery fired on enemy trenches in retaliation for PIPSQUEAK firing at trench near V.1.
9.10.a.m. 20th Battery registered communication trench leading from S. of P.11 to German front trench.
9.15.a.m. 2nd Battery registered point on German trench 50 yds S. of R.8.
10.55.a.m. and 12.25.p.m. 2nd Battery fired on PIPSQUEAK Battery which was subsequently engaged effectively by 23th Heavy Battery observation from LEICESTER LOUNGE.
11.30.a.m. and 6.10.p.m. 44th Battery registered new gun positions in N.52.c.10.9, occupied last night.
*11.55.a.m. 8th Siege Battery fired one round at battery which was active from N.35.a.1.5. 45th Heavy Battery then took it on.
*12.25.p.m. 8th Siege Battery fired two rounds at P.10.4.9 (WARNETON) — no activity visible and so ceased firing.
2.15.p.m. 8th Battery fired at a house about K.20 which appeared to be used as an O.P.
4.10.p.m. 8th Battery fired at trench R.8.a.15 in retaliation for shelling of our own trenches.
*6.25.p.m. 8th Siege Battery fired 6 rounds at hostile battery whose flashes were observed at A.8.b.4.0.
WESTUBERT was being shelled from direction of VIOLAINES at this time.
*10th Siege Battery was engaged and was on trench R.3.d.7.2. in preparation of attack by 7th Division.
(4.p.m. to 6.p.m. 3 Batteries of 4th Brigade R.F.A. registered with (operations of 4th Corps in view commenced bombardment of:-
((i)   L.17 trench junction L.17.d.
((ii) Aide communication way
Special((iii) Vicinity L.11, L.12, L.13.
Task (7.p.m. to 8.p.m. a very slow rate of fire as mentioned on above tasks
     (by request of 7th Divisional Artillery.
4th (9.p.m. to 9.30.p.m. Above operation was repeated (20 rounds per battery)
Brigade(10.p.m. to 2.a.m. 4th June 1915.
R.F.A. (1 Battery 4th Brigade fired occasional rounds every 5 mins on L.17 and
       (approaches.
       (1 Battery 4th Brigade fired occasionally on trenches R.8 and L.13.
9.25.p.m. 2nd Battery retaliated on enemy trenches at request of Infantry as our trenches were being heavily shelled.
(* Information furnished by)

(b) ACTION BY HEAVY ARTILLERY:

9.30.p.m. 2nd heavy battery fired 15 rounds on enemy trench at
heavy howitzer shelled ARGAPY.

4th June 1915.

8.a.m. 12.a.m. howitzer

9.10 a.m.
12 noon. Heavy battery and 2nd Battery shelled communication trenches from P.8 to DUTTIES and also on German trenches from direction of BEAU PUITS.
12.45.p.m. ITALIAN and 61st Batteries fired on trenches in P.10.
12.51.p.m. 12 inch howitzer engaged enemy battery and some rounds N. of BRENAKI's WOOD.
1.30.p.m. PIPSQUEAK shelled
communication
2.8. to 3.p.m. howitzer
demolition of LOMBAR.
4.10.p.m. to 5.p.m. howitzer
1st and 2nd line trenches
afternoon.

APPENDIX 235(a)

No G-116.

Headquarters Meerut Division.

3rd June 1915.

Copy of a memo. from Indian Corps to Meerut Division, No G-615, dated 2nd June 1915.

-:-:-:-:-:-:-:-:-:-:-:-:-:-

Early

From information received in this office it appears that the following expenditure of ammunition was incurred by your Division on the dates mentioned:-

	18-pr.	
	H.E.	Shrapnel.
29th May.	153.	694.
30th May.	136.	303.
31st May.	293.	561.
1st June.	72.	757.

In view of the necessity for economy in ammunition and especially H.E. which has repeatedly been intimated, please furnish for the information of the Corps Commander full details of how this expenditure was incurred.

Until further orders no H.E. for any description of gun is to be used except in cases of most urgent necessity, or for a definite operation which has received the concurrence of the Corps Commander.

The Corps Commander feels sure that it will not be necessary for him to call attention again to this matter.

-:-:-:-:-:e:-

MEMORANDUM.

For information and report please.

Colonel.
General Staff.
MEERUT DIVISION.

To:-

C. R. A. MEERUT.

APPENDIX 235(B)

No.708-R.A.(L).   Headquarters Divisional Artillery,
                              MEERUT DIVISION.

                              3rd June 1915.

To,

   The GENERAL STAFF.

      MEERUT DIVISION.

Reference your G-116 of date.

By order of the MEERUT Division during the days under reference 29th May to 1st June, the following trenches were slowly and systematically bombarded by deliberate observed fire, 100 rounds H.E. and shrapnel (about ½ and ½) being allotted to each task:-

   V.2. and trenches in immediate vicinity.
   V.2. to R.8.
   R.8. to 200 yards W.

This entailed an expenditure of H.E. of roughly 150 rounds a day.

On May the 31st 293 rounds of H.E. were expended. This was abnormal and was caused by an order from the Division for 4 batteries to bombard at 12.15.a.m. and 2.15.a.m., parapets damaged during the previous day. During the bombardment each gun fired 6 shrapnel and 4 H.E. on each occasion.

The remaining expenditure of shrapnel referred to in your No.G-116 was incurred in carrying out the operations as detailed in my progress report of the day's in question. Constant moves ordered in taking over new portions of the line entail the expenditure of much ammunition as registering becomes necessary. A great saving in ammunition would automatically follow if such moves were curtailed.

I would like to bring the following points to notice.

After the action of NEUVE CHAPELLE till 9th May our expenditure of ammunition was cut down to a minimum- result being the enemy was at liberty to build up and strengthen his works without molestation. The Germans took full advantage of this and so built their parapets that practically no impression was made on them by our bombardment on 9th May 1915.

Bearing

APPENDIX 236

SECRET.

TACTICAL PROGRESS REPORT
4th June 1915.

1(a) ACTION BY OUR OWN ARTILLERY.

8.40.p.m. 3rd June 1915. 2nd Battery fired a salvo at the enemy's trenches in retaliation, at request of O.C. 4th Seaforth's, which had desired effect.
4th June 1915:-
9.55.a.m. 2nd Battery fired at enemy's trenches in retaliation.
11.a.m. 8th Battery fired at trench R.8. where germans were seen.
11.15.a.m. 26th Battery registered ORCHARD near P.18 and house between P.18 and Q.12.
11.30.a.m. 19th Battery registered trench Q.12-Q.15.
12.45.p.m. 2nd Battery fired at farm near P.18 to check registration.
1.40.p.m. 8th Siege Battery engaged T 19 c 2'9 in response to shelling of First Aid Post and S 2 c. Direct hit on house just over LORGIES Church at 2nd round.
1.55.p.m. Above batteries again active, 8th Siege Battery fired 4 rounds of lyddite and batteries then ceased firing.
4.p.m. 8th Battery registered on R.10 and FERME de TOULOTTE.
5.50.p.m. 2nd Battery registered house with 2 loopholes high up at or near N.24, which is obviously an O.P.; it is visible from LEICESTER LOUNGE and is probably worth some heavy ammunition.

(b) ACTION BY HOSTILE ARTILLERY.

10.30.a.m. 21.c.m. howitzer shelled vicinity of X 18 c for about 1½ hour
11.10.a.m. 15.c.m. howitzer shelled house at S 21 c 9'3, mentioned as likely ranging point in yesterday's Tactical Progress Report(last para).
11.45.a.m. 15.c.m. howitzer shelled RICHEBOURG for about an hour, including 7th and 14th Battery positions. Direction of LORGIES indicated.
12.15.p.m. Infantry reserve near N.2. shelled by howitzers from direction of DISTILLERY.
12.15.p.m. PIPSQUEAK shelled vicinity of S 8 a and S 7 b. PIPSQUEAK shelled CHOCOLAT MENIER CORNER(S 14 b 7'4).
1.4.p.m. St VAAST post heavily shelled by heavy howitzers(15.c.m. ? 21. c.m.) direction LORGIES.
2.30.p.m. PIPSQUEAK shelled reserve trenches East of INDIAN VILLAGE.
3.p.m. 15.c.m. howitzer shelled new communication trench N.11-P.11 from direction of LA RUSSIE. Was silenced by 4th Brigade R.G.A.
4.30.p.m. 21.c.m. howitzer shelled vicinity of X 18 c.
6.15.p.m. 15.c.m. howitzer shelled RUE de l'EPINETTE for ½ an hour, beginning just W. of INDIAN VILLAGE S 20 a and searching back to road.
6.45.p.m. 21.c.m. howitzer shelled vicinity S 8 a 4'4.
8.1.p.m. 6th Battery, South of RICHEBOURG, shelled by PIPSQUEAKS from direction of VIOLAINES.
10.p.m. A few PIPSQUEAKS falling in RICHEBOURG

2. INFORMATION.

SEARCHLIGHT:- Bearing of searchlight taken last night from X 18 a 4'8 varied from 77° to 97°, which points to it being on some form of travelling carriage.
AIRCRAFT:- 6.50.p.m. Hostile bi-plane over NEUVE CHAPELLE-observing German aeroplane passed over RUE du BOIS three times between 6.30.p.m. and 7.p.m. - it was seen to release carrier pigeons.
LIGHTS:- Two VEREY's lights sent up true bearing 14°40' from M 33 a 3'7 at 9.30.p.m. Two flares sent up similar to those used by Germans N.W. of CROIX BARBEE at 9.15.p.m.
PROBABLE O.P.:- See para 1(a) 5.50.p.m. above.

Major R.

Brigade Major, Royal Artillery,
MEERUT DIVISION.

SECRET.   War Diary APPENDIX 237
                                                                                              12

                    L I A S O N   B A R R A G E S
              M E E R U T   D I V I S I O N A L   A R T I L L E R Y.

1 F   13th Brigade R.F.A. front is attacked(LAHORE DIVISION-SOUTHERN SECTION)

          13th Brigade R.F.A..........Barrage C.13 to C.12 and C.17 to C.18 to
                                           C.14.

1 F   13th Brigade R.F.A. front is attacked(MEERUT DIVISION-NORTHERN SECTION-
       DEHRA DUN BRIGADE

          13th Brigade R.F.A..........Barrage C.20-C.19-C.11, and R.18-R.6.
          (LAHORE Divisional Artillery)
                                                  (G Battery R.14-R.13-R.12.
          9th Brigade R.F.A...........Barrage   (1 Battery C.19-C.18.
                                                  (1 Battery covered 9th FFG ridge's
                                                  (own front.

1 F   9th Brigade R.F.A. front is attacked (MEERUT DIVISION - CENTRE SECTION
       BAREILLY BRIGADE.

          13th Brigade R.F.A..........Barrage C.13-C.12-C.17, also C.9, C.14,
                                           C.18.

          2nd HIGHLAND Brigade R.F.A..Barrage on its T.18-   and R.11-R.12

  F   2nd HIGHLAND Brigade R.F.A. front is attacked(MEERUT DIVISION - SOUTHERN
       SOUTHERN SECTION.

          9th Brigade R.F.A...........Barrage on enemy's front attack lines

       Night lines of 58th Howitzer Battery R.F.A. in the above barrages are as
       follows:-

              1 gun on Orchard and front
              1 gun on cross-roads
              1 gun on
              2 guns on cross roads to

"A" Form.   Army Form C. 2121.

MESSAGES AND SIGNALS.

No. of Message 238

Prefix SR Code DSP m. Words 95 Charge   APPENDIX   Recd. at 4.5 P.m.
Priority   Sent   Date 4/6/15
                 At ..... m.   From
                 To ......   By Chapman
                 By

TO — CRA Meerut

Sender's Number: G164
Day of Month: 4th
In reply to Number:
AAA

Following from Indian Corps for information begins G654 4th 30th How Battery is a replaced at disposal of OC 43rd How Bde addressed Meerut repeated Lahore Ends

From / Place: Meerut
Time: 4 Pm

"A" Form. Army Form C.
MESSAGES AND SIGNALS. No. of Message

Prefix S_ Code C I P m | Words 65 | Charge | This message is on a/c of: | Recd. at 23 _ m.
Office of Origin and Service Instructions. | Sent | | APPENDIX 23 | Date
YIG Priority | At ___ m. To ___ By ___ | | Service. (Signature of "Franking Officer.") | From ___ By ___

TO — ~~H ay~~ ARTY
Meerut DIVN

Sender's Number.	Day of Month.	In reply to Number	AAA
* G 184	5th		

Under instructions of first Army Meerut Div is to place 1 Field Artillery Bde at disposal of Indian Corp temporary for tactical purposes AAA 9th Bde RFA selected AAA Please arrange details in direct communication with 7th Div Arty Addressed Meerut Div Arty repeated Indian Corp 7th Div 4th Corps Reference

From Indian Corp G 667
Place
Time

The above may be forwarded as now corrected. (Z) Meerut ___
Censor. | Signature of Addresser or person authorised to telegraph in his name.
* This line should be erased if not required.

"A" Form. Army Form C. 2121.
MESSAGES AND SIGNALS.

Prefix SM Code CKA m Words 68 Charge
Office of ... and Service Instructions. YIG

This message is on a/c of APPENDIX 240 Recd. at 4·0 a.m. Date F I G 5/6/15 From YIG By G. Woulao?

TO — CRA MEERUT

Sender's Number: *G-187 Day of Month: 5th In reply to Number: AAA

Indian corps wire begins G-668 of date AAA Please place one section 4·5 Howt at disposal of Meerut Div together with proportion of ammunition scholar AAA Section Officer to report to CRA Meerut today for orders AAA All details of movements to be arranged by 8th and Meerut Divs direct Addressed 8th Div Repeated Meerut Div ends for information

From: MEERUT DIV
Time: 3·40 PM

APPENDIX 241

SECRET.

TACTICAL PROGRESS REPORT
8th June 1915.

1(a) ACTION BY OUR OWN ARTILLERY.
2.45.a.m. 18th Battery fired on working party at F.17 and disturbed them.
3.p.m. 8th Battery registered earthworks near G.13.
4.5.p.m. 2nd Battery registered N.27 suspected as being an O.P., as men seen leaving it and two horses grazing near.
5.42.p.m. MOTHER fired 2 rounds at LA RUSSIE battery "by request" owing to report of howitzer shelling "B" and C. action trenches from that direction.
44th Battery registered FERME de TOUROTTE and FERME du BOIS during the day.
House N.24 reported in yesterday's Tactical Progress Report as likely O.P. was taken on to-day by MOTHER- 1st round hit the corner and several germans were seen bolting; 2nd round just over; 3rd round plump into middle of house.

(b) ACTION BY HOSTILE ARTILLERY.
4.a.m. RITZ and vicinity shelled by PIPSQUEAK.-
4.45.a.m.   do.   do.   do.
12 noon. 21.c.m. howitzer shelled vicinity of N.12 a- firing about 6 rounds.
2.10.p.m., to 3.p.m.- and vicinity of O.P. were heavily shelled. At 4.30.p.m. fire was switched
4.30.p.m. to 4.50.p.m.   on to the TRENCHES (B.4.) Infantry
                                        report these trenches badly damaged.
3.45.p.m. PIPSQUEAK shelled RUE de l'EPINETTE. 10.c.m. howitzer shelled vicinity K.3 a.b. about 1½ hours.
4.p.m. 10.5.c.m. howitzer shelled vicinity of K.17 c for a quarter of an hour.
5.p.m. to 6.p.m. (ex 15-c.m.)howitzer shelled our right trenches in vicinity of S.21.b from direction of LA BASSEE.
5.30.p.m.   shelled B.4 trenches for considerable time.
5.25.p.m. PIPSQUEAK and 10-cm. fired from RUE T'ILBECQ. WOOD on to RUE de l'EPINETTE.
6.30.p.m. PIPSQUEAK shelled TROU LE MORIN CROSSROADS (K.17.d).

2. INFORMATION.
AIRCRAFT:- Between 10.a.m. and 12.30.p.m. a number of reports were received regarding hostile aeroplanes being in the air. Shelled by our fire. From the ground at the vicinity of RICHEBOURG L'AVOUE were three hostile aeroplanes flying very high. At 11.15.a.m. they were chased by our Archibalds. A report at the same time stated a bomb or two had been dropped and flown away.
3.45.p.m. Hostile biplane flying high east of vicinity of FERME du RITZ but fairly low- was reported quite badly. Towards heavy howitzer was shelling aerodrome at this time. Archibalds reported shooting very short.
8.30.a.m. Hostile sausage balloon from bearing 110° from P.10. Gr K.13. went down at 10.30.a.m. and was up 11.30.at 10.40.a.m. and down again at 1.10.p.m.
11.30.a.m. Civilian balloon observed just behind German lines N.15. 217.- disappeared at 1.30.p.m.- Observed another balloon went down at 1.30.p.m.
4.p.m. Sausage observed from bearing 108°

SECRET.

APPENDIX 242

TACTICAL PROGRESS REPORT
6th June 1915.

1(a) ACTION BY OUR OWN ARTILLERY.

8.15.a.m. 2nd Battery fired at Germans seen near V.4.
1.30.p.m. 20th Battery registered trench L.11-L.12 and all conspicuous points in vicinity of RUE d'OUVERT, also houses on road running towards M.8. and part of trench running out towards L.10.
1.40.p.m. 19th Battery registered trenches in vicinity of L.12.
2.40.p.m. 2nd Battery fired at suspected O.P.-M.27.
2.46.p.m. 2nd Battery engaged PIPSQUEAK near S 23 c 9'9.
3.p.m. 28th Battery registered VIOLAINES, K.24. houses at L.13 and L.11 points L.12, M.14, K.12, trench L.11-L.13-L.10.
3.30.p.m. 8th Battery fired at trench 800 yards E. of FERME de TOULOTTE.
4.35.p.m. and 5.15.p.m. 14th Battery fired 2 rounds on enemy's trenches in retaliation for our own trenches being shelled.
4.55.p.m. 8th Battery fired 3 salvos on trench R.B. to Q.16. in retaliation.
5.30.p.m. 2nd, 8th, 44th, 14th and 68th Batteries R.F.A. carried out combined shoot with MOTHER on houses S.W. of Q.14 - a few rounds only fired.
6.p.m. 2nd Battery fired to stop PIPSQUEAK at S 23 c 9'9 with good result.
8.15.p.m. 14th Battery fired on german trenches as their artillery fired on our support trenches.
Batteries of 4th Brigade R.F.A. carried out registration during the day.

(b) ACTION BY HOSTILE ARTILLERY.
7.10.p.m. 5th June 1915. PIPSQUEAK fired 3 salvos on our front trenches in vicinity of P.11 immediately followed by heavy howitzers in same vicinity.
6th June 1915:-
10.45.a.m. 10.5.c.m. howitzer shelled our support trenches in vicinity of N.9. from direction of VIOLAINES.
10.45.a.m. 15.c.m. howitzer shelled vicinity S 19 d from direction of BEAU PUITS.
11.30.a.m. 15.c.m. howitzer shelled vicinity of X 16 c.
1.p.m. PIPSQUEAK and 10.5.c.m. howitzer shelled 1st and 2nd line trenches of "A" Sub-section. Fire was reported very accurate and was continued for considerable period. aeroplane reports battery at T 21 b. culprit.

5.45.p.m. 15.c.m. howitzer shelled vicinity X 18 a and cross roads X 18 c 10'7 for one hour and obtained direct hits on roads X 18 c 10'7. There were several "bursts" of hostile fire on our first line trench near P.10 during the afternoon.

2. INFORMATION.
AIRCRAFT:- 4 p.m. Sausage balloon near the S. of square O.6 c.
7.p.m. German "wireless" plane was up.
MOVEMENT:- About 12 noon several germans were seen moving about in trench in front of FERME du BOIS, 60 yards S. of R.5 and N. of Q.15.
7.12.p.m. Good deal of movement in communication trench from V.6a to V.6e, chiefly at end nearest the RITZ.
GENERAL:- 5.45 p.m. 4th Brigade R.F.A. having completed its new registration, took over Artillery support of Gaddiff's Brigade front from 8th Brigade R.F.A., which was then temporarily placed at the disposal of the 4th Corps by order of G.O.C.
10.p.m. Reported that GUNS were heard in the "Chapel" near S.4.d

P.T.O

APPENDIX 243

S E C R E T.

TACTICAL PROGRESS REPORT
7th June 1915.

1(a) ACTION BY OUR OWN ARTILLERY.
11.45.p.m., 12.30.a.m. No. ... Battery fired on German working parties
12.45.a.m. Night 6th/7th June|parties at FERME COUR d'AVOINE. Infantry reported not molested.

7th June 1915:-
8.a.m. and 11.55.a.m. 66th Battery fired on German working parties at COUR d'AVOINE in retaliation on enemy shelling our trenches.
10.18.a.m. 14th Battery fired on enemy trenches in retaliation to enemy's batteries firing on our trenches.
11.a.m. 44th Battery fired at points near FERME COUR d'AVOINE and at ruins indicated by ... in ... on ... in the foreground.
12.30.p.m. 14th Battery fired on working party at ...
1.p.m. 44th Battery registered farm or ... on points and two localities S.E. of FERME COUR d'AVOINE.
4.15.p.m. 66th Battery registered trench X 28 a 6/9 to 9 29 a 9/9.
4.30.p.m. 9th Battery completed registration on trench at hill.
5.p.m. 66th Battery fired 4 cartridges at GOM'S ... (a probable O.P.).
7th battery carried out registration ... the following ... eleven points being registered.
J.20, K.7, X.19, A 4 a ..., 9.29 a ..., 9.29 a ...
Attempts to continue registering with accurate fuzes during were not successful, owing to difficulties of reading the lens.
Section of 66th Battery ... ... of registration by percussion shrapnel ...

(b) ACTION BY HOSTILE ARTILLERY.
9.45.a.m. to 10.45.a.m. German ... fired 20 ... rounds at ... yards of 7th Battery now quitting. At least 2 of ... fuzes bursting near the battery- no damage.
10.45.a.m. ... ...
10.45.a.m. PRESQUAY ... ... houses close to O.P. ... ...
during morning- casualty ... ... points
11.15.a.m. PERNEQUAY ... ...
1.15.p.m. 12 ... ... lightly ... ... for about ½ hour. During the morning ... ... our trenches in vicinity.

2. INFORMATION.
AIRCRAFT:
enemy aeroplane at ... ... on the ... of ... ...

S E C R E T.   TACTICAL   PROGRESS   REPORT   APPENDIX 244
                            8th June 1915.

1(a) ACTION BY OUR OWN ARTILLERY.
   Observation very difficult to-day.
   6.45.a.m. and 12.5.p.m. 14th Battery fired a few rounds on enemy's trenches in retaliation to enemy shelling ours.
   11.15.a.m. 66th Battery fired on enemy's trenches in reply to PIPSQUEAK firing on our reserve trenches.
   1.50.p.m. 8th Battery fired on R.8 - Q.16 in retaliation.
   2.p.m. 2nd Battery fired on night lines in retaliation.
   2.15.p.m. 2nd Battery fired to stop enemy bombing our trenches near V.2. Bombing ceased.
   4.20.p.m. and 5.40.p.m. 2nd Battery registered V.3 to R.8 as new night line.
   5.30.p.m. to 6.30.p.m. 7th Battery registered L.11 - L.12 and Salient to West.
   Section of 55th Howitzer Battery registered FERME du BOIS and trench in front, also farm near P.18 during the day.

(b) ACTION BY HOSTILE ARTILLERY.
   6.30.a.m. PIPSQUEAK shelled in front of 14th and 66th Batteries (South of RICHEBOURG).
   5.30.p.m. PIPSQUEAK shelled INDIAN VILLAGE (S.20).
   5.50.p.m. PIPSQUEAK active on roads in S 2 c.
   6.p.m. PIPSQUEAK shelled vicinity X 18 a and X 18 c.
   8.45.p.m. PIPSQUEAK fired a few shell N.W. of RICHEBOURG.
   HIGHLAND Division trenches were shelled throughout the day, as a result of their bombardment of enemy trenches and wire.

2.   INFORMATION.
   AIRCRAFT:- 9.25.a.m. Hostile aeroplane over LA COUTURE - returned over PORT ARTHUR at 9.30.a.m. - back again over our lines at 9.41.a.m.
   6.45.p.m. German bi-plane up over RICHEBOURG.
   LIGHTS:- Between 10.30.p.m. and midnight 7th June a lamp appeared from time to time bearing 190° from "SAVOY"(S 9 c 5'0); at same time intermittent lights were observed from direction of RICHEBOURG or LA COUTURE.
   About 4.30.p.m. 8th June- Two white lights seen to go up in vicinity of S 20 d and immediately afterwards the Germans shelled the whole of that locality for about three quarters of an hour. At this time a considerable number of Infantry were moving up from RUE de l'EPINETTE to INDIAN VILLAGE.

                                                   Major R.A.
                                        Brigade Major, Royal Artillery,
                                               MEERUT DIVISION.

FOLLOWING REPORT FROM 4th BRIGADE R.G.A. OPERATING ON MEERUT DIVISION FRONT:-

Following batteries engaged during day:-

10.10.a.m. S 29 b 4'4 reported active and stopped.
10.50.a.m. S 30 central believed active.
11.18.a.m. Howitzer behind house at A 6 a 7'7.) This howitzer stops on
11.53.a.m.   do.   do.   do.   ) being engaged, but re-opens
2.38.p.m.   do.   do.   do.   ) later.
4.42.p.m.   do.   do.   do.   )
2.20.p.m. S 29 b 4'4.
4.55.p.m. Flashes seen at A 6 a 8'1 - engaged by 48th Heavy Battery and soon stopped.
5.42.p.m. S 29 b 8'8 believed active.
6.35.p.m. Flashes seen at .... with success.

FOLLOWING REPORT FROM 1st BRIGADE R.G.A. OPERATING ON MEERUT DIVISION FRONT:-

5.45.p.m. 8th Siege Battery fired 5 rounds at T 25 a 1'4 and T 31 b 5'4 in reply to shelling of our trenches.
7.p.m. 8th Siege Bos.3 and 4 guns Mark VII fired a few rounds registration on trench in front of RUE d'OUVERT in neighbourhood of K.W.
MOTHER resting and standing by for N.F. targets from aeroplane to be received.

"A" Form. Army Form C. 2121.

MESSAGES AND SIGNALS.

No. of Message

Prefix ____ Code ____ m Words 52 Charge ____ APPENDIX 24 Rec'd at 11.13 p.m.
Office of Origin and Service Instructions.   This message is on a/c of :-   Date 7/6/15
Sent At ____ m. ____ Service. From VG
To ____   By O.Krumpelt
By ____ (Signature of "Franking Officer.")

TO — C R A

Sender's Number. Q3/128   Day of Month. 7th   In reply to Number   AAA

Indian Corps wires begins AAA
Return received here shows an
expenditure of 618 rds of 18 pdr
Shrapnel fired by your division
during 24 hours ending noon today
AAA Please furnish details of
how expended ends AAA For
early report

From Meerut Divn
Place
Time

The above may be forwarded as now corrected. (Z)

Censor. Signature of Addressor or person authorised to telegraph in his name.
* This line should be erased if not required.

Amm: File.

APPENDIX. 246

No. S.C.6

Headquarters Divisional Artillery,
MEERUT DIVISION.

8th June 1915.

To,

The A.A. & Q.M.G.,
MEERUT DIVISION.

With reference to your No.Q-3/128 dated the 7th instant, the figures given are correct.

322 of the 618 rounds were fired by the 9th Brigade R.F.A. under orders of 7th Division for which no responsibility can be accepted by the MEERUT Division.

The remaining 296 rounds were fired as follows:-

     133 by 4th Brigade R.F.A.

     163 by 13th Brigade R.F.A.

The objectives engaged are reported in Tactical Progress Report, MEERUT Divisional Artillery of date asked for in your No.Q-3/128. Owing to orders from superior authority being received to place 9th Brigade R.F.A. at disposal of 4th Corps instead of 4th Brigade R.F.A. as previously arranged by MEERUT Division, re-registration became necessary, and ammunition for this purpose was expended by 4th Brigade R.F.A. as they then became responsible for front of BAREILLY Brigade vice 9th Brigade R.F.A. transferred to 4th Corps.

Brigadier General, R.A.
Commanding Royal Artillery, MEERUT Division.

APPENDIX 24

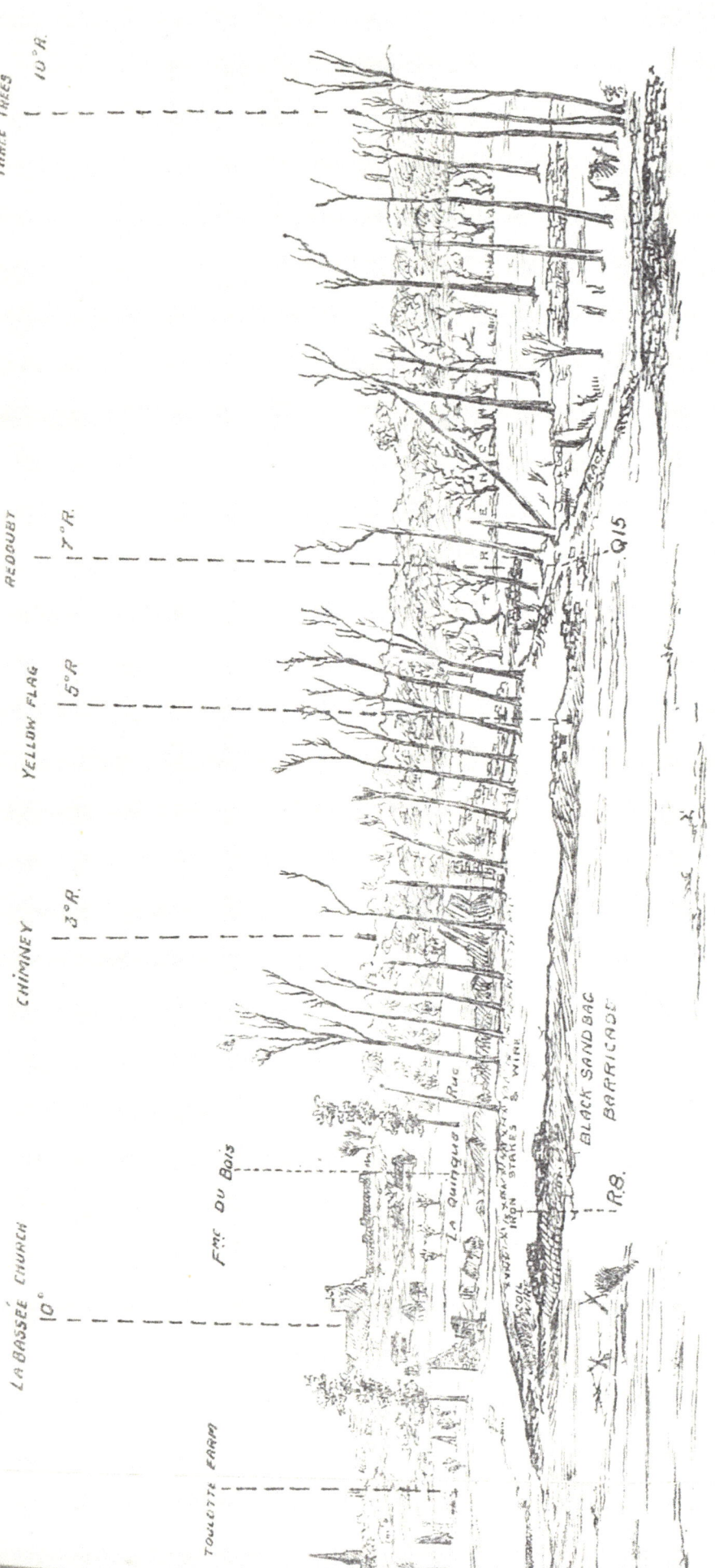

S E C R E T   TACTICAL   PROGRESS   REPORT   APPENDIX 248
                               8th June 1915.
                    ****

(a) ACTION BY OUR OWN ARTILLERY:
    12.55.a.m. 14th Battery fired at Bomb Gun N. of P.14 at request of
    Infantry.
    8.40.a.m. 8th Battery fired on Germans working in the open 300 yards
    N.W. of P.18.
    10.5.a.m. to 11.a.m. 46th Battery fired at intervals on our trenches
    in retaliation to german guns firing on our front line trenches.
    10.30.a.m. and 4.p.m. 7th Battery retaliated when enemy shelled our
    11.30.a.m. 8th Battery retaliated on enemy's trenches for shelling our
    front line behind V.8. and our support trench behind V.1.
    11.25.a.m., 11.45.a.m., 11.50.a.m., 2nd Battery retaliated on enemy's
    3.40.p.m., 4.15.p.m., 4.25.p.m.   front trenches for shelling ours.
    and 4.27.p.m.
    11.45.a.m. 14th Battery fired a few rounds on working party near Q.8.
    12.10.p.m. 7th Battery fired a few rounds on German trenches.
    4.30.p.m. 8th Battery fired a few rounds on V.2. to Q.8. and at ruined
    cottage near Q.12.
    8.30.p.m. 8th Battery shelled enemy's trenches for 1 hour in reply
    to hostile shelling of our trenches by HOWITZER.

(b) ACTION BY HOSTILE ARTILLERY.
    8.45.a.m. 15.c.m. howitzer shelled vicinity S.22.c.
    10.5.a.m. to 11.a.m. PIPSQUEAKS shelled our support trenches intermitt-
    ently.
    11.20.a.m. Intermittent shelling on our front line behind V.8. and on
    our support trench behind V.1. A few yards short Y.13.c.
    11.45.a.m. and 2.40.p.m. PIPSQUEAK active on our trenches.
    1.50.p.m. PIPSQUEAK fired a few rounds on road in front of 14th battery
    position (S.2.c).
    3.20.p.m. PIPSQUEAK fired at junction of road S. of RICHEBOURG.
    3.30.p.m. Enemy shelled house at S.3.c.5'4 with 9.c.m. howitzer-getting
    3 direct hits.
    15.c.m. howitzer shelled N.W. of RICHEBOURG and in the region of the
    RITZ.
    4.p.m. PIPSQUEAK shelled support trenches near the FORTH BRIDGE vigor-
    ously.
    4.3.p.m. Light howitzer shelled RICHEBOURG(large report say 21.c.m.)
    8.30.p.m. PIPSQUEAK shelled support trenches on LANDED BRIGADE
    heavily.

    INFORMATION.
    AIRCRAFT:- Following hostile aeroplanes were up to-day:-
    One up over S.20.c.10'2 at 4.15.a.m.
    One up over S.21.a.6'7 at 5.30.a.m.
    One up over battery at S.20.b at 6.30.a.m.
    One very high over RICHEBOURG observation and found line lights at
    8.40.a.m. Hostile howitzer immediately opened fire on our HIGHLAND
    batteries causing some casualties.

    BOMBING:- 10.45.a.m. Our infantry bombed trenches at V.1. and V.8.

                                                      Major R.A.
                                      Brigade Major, Royal Artillery,
                                                EIGHTH DIVISION.

FOLLOWING REPORT FROM 4th DIVISION R.F.A. REPORTING ON FOURTH DIVISION FRONT:-

Observation difficult. All day the Brigade took on the following tar-
batteries etc:-
8.55.a.m. (S.24.b.4'4 active, but doing no damage and not engaged.
1.50.p.m. Group report our trenches at I.4. being heavily shelled by
engaged G.28.c.5'4 reported active and engaged.
3.5.p.m. "PALACE" shelled and RICHEBOURG reported by
3.30 central- S.24.b.6'9 and LORGIES.("PALACE" is RICHEBOURG Church.)
6.23.p.m. R.F.A. MEERUT Division reported our trenches at RUINOUS HOUSES
shelled from PEAU PUITS-VIOLAINES. Opened on P.19.a.6'2, P.19.a.ruined and
fired with orders to continue on VIOLAINES of shelling continued.

"A" Form.   Army Form C. 2121.
MESSAGES AND SIGNALS.   No. of Message

Prefix	Code HP m	Words 61	Charge	This message is on a/c of:	Recd. at 8-1 m.
Office of Origin and Service Instructions. TRG	Sent At m. To By			Service. (Signature of "Franking Officer.")	Date 10/6/15 From 415 By E. Bryant
Priority					

TO — C R A Meerut

Sender's Number. S-324	Day of Month. 10th	In reply to Number	A A A

Indian Corps wire series G-737 of date aaa 19th Divn will place one Bty of 5 inch howitzer at disposal of 8th Divn aaa Meerut Divn will place section of 55th Howitzer Bty at disposal of Indian Divn aaa details of movements where necessary to be arranged between Divnl Cmdrs direct aaa ends

From
Place   Meerut Dick
Time   7.05 pm

The above may be forwarded as now corrected.   (Z)

Censor.   Signature of Addresser or person authorised to telegraph in his name.

* This line should be erased if not required.

SECRET.

APPENDIX 250

TACTICAL PROGRESS REPORT
10th June 1915.

1(a) ACTION BY OUR OWN ARTILLERY.
9th June 1915:-
7.35.p.m. 7th Battery fired a few rounds at enemy trenches at request of Infantry in reply to shelling of our own trenches.
8.8.p.m. 2nd Battery retaliated on trench V.2 to R.8.
8.16.p.m. to 8.40.p.m. 2nd Battery retaliated on trench V.2 to R.8.
8.30.p.m. to 8.50.p.m. 8th Battery retaliated on trench R.8 to Q.13.
10th June 1915:-
9.5.a.m., 10.35.a.m. and 4.45.p.m. 36th Battery retaliated on enemy trenches.

(b) ACTION BY HOSTILE ARTILLERY.
PIPSQUEAK shelled vicinity of RUE du BOIS, LA COUTURE, VEILLE CHAPELLE and PONT du HEM with a few rounds during the day.
12 noon. 10.5.c.m. Howitzers shelled LA COUTURE for about two hours, firing one round every ten minutes.
3.p.m. Same battery(probably) shelled KING's ROAD(X 11), true bearing of report 104° from X 18 a 4'5.
5.15.p.m. to 7.p.m. Same battery(probably) switched down to LE TOURET- firing at intervals.
Two light shell fell in the neighbourhood of Chateau at LA CROIX MARMEUSE during the afternoon- one was blind.

2. INFORMATION.
A very quiet dull day.
AIRCRAFT:- No hostile aircraft reported.

R.H. Lynch-Staunton.
Major R.A.
Brigade Major, Royal Artillery,
MEERUT DIVISION.

FOLLOWING REPORT FROM 1st BRIGADE R.G.A. OPERATING ON MEERUT DIVISION FRONT

A very quiet day. 8th Siege fired 5 lyddite into VIOLAINES in response to shelling of VEILLE CHAPELLE.

FOLLOWING REPORT FROM 4th BRIGADE R.G.A. OPERATING ON MEERUT DIVISION FRONT

9.p.m. 9th June 1915:- PIPSQUEAK continually active behind DISTILLERY in S 17 a. 48th engaged S 17 b 4'2 and shut him up.
10th June 1915:-
8.45.a.m. 48th Heavy Battery fired a few rounds at S 17 b 4'2 and S 24 b 2'2 as PIPSQUEAK occasionally active in the mist.
1.15.p.m. O.P. PALACE report Howitzer firing on LA COUTURE from close range- not located.
2.10.p.m. Engaged S 11 d 3'3 and S 24 b 0'10 as enemy's battery shelling VEILLE CHAPELLE.
2.25.p.m. Engaged S 24 b 3'4 and S 24 b 10'1 reported active.
3.5.p.m. BEAU PUITS Batteries active-engaged S 30 b 2'1 and S 30 b 4'3 searching and sweeping for the offenders.
3.10.p.m. O.P. PALACE reported howitzer shelling VEILLE CHAPELLE has ceased firing- probably this gun was run up close owing to the mist as it appeared to be very near but could not locate it.
Very difficult to locate enemy's active batteries.

APPENDIX 251
(5 pages)

No.730-R.A.(L).   Headquarters Divisional Artillery,
                   MEERUT DIVISION.

                   10th June 1915.

To,

   The Brigadier General, Royal Artillery.
        INDIAN CORPS.

Sir,

   In reply to your memorandum dated the 8th June 1915,
I have the honour to submit herewith my experiences and opinions
on the various points mentioned:-

OBJECTIVE.   The choice of objective should be suitable to
Artillery preparation and concentration of Artillery on it.

WIRE CUTTING.   At wire stretched taut between uprights, a
frontal fire from a range averaging 2000 yards with shrapnel
burst close up to the wire to be cut will prove effective.
A successful method was found to be to concentrate the guns of
a half battery on the same gap, thus by allotting a frontage of
100 yards to one battery, two points are selected on this front,
each with 3 guns bearing on the same point, this will ensure two
complete gaps being made and the experience of NEUVE CHAPELLE
was to show that most of the wire between the gaps aimed at
was also shot away.   Careful registration on the day of
operations, good platforms and anchoring the guns are very
necessary adjuncts.   Observation should preferably be from
the front trenches.

Wire which is not taut, such as French wire in hoops, is a much
more difficult obstacle to destroy, in as much as there is not
the same resistance to the bullets.   I am inclined to believe
H.E. would be the more effective projectile at this objective,
and concentrated fire converging on the front of wire meant to
be destroyed should have the necessary effect.

I am of opinion, though cannot speak from personal experience,
that the 2" trench mortars firing a 60 lb. shell with a range of
                                                    500 yards

800 yards, could be advantageously used to destroy this hoop wire, provided the ground where the wire rests is not too soft, otherwise a very deep crater is made, which may in turn become a serious obstacle to our Infantry, but on average ground in dry weather such a crater will not be made, and above defect will not exist.

1st LINE TRENCHES. Now as the lines of enemy's trenches are strong breastworks heavily sand bagged, I consider the only way of dealing with them effectively is to bombard them with heavy Howitzers viz: 6" and 9'2" Howitzers if safe, systematically till they cease to become a serious obstacle. When this has been accomplished thoroughly, the assault can be delivered. I am against the attack being ordered until the enemy's defences are considered to have been sufficiently demolished. This can only be determined by actual observation from the most suitable observing station obtainable for this purpose, and presumably the opinion of the Artillery on this point (in conjunction, if possible, with that of the Infantry Commander of the attack) ~~the point~~, would be the best available.

2nd LINE TRENCHES. Require to be dealt with much in the same manner as the first line trenches. If owing to proximity of our own fire trenches to those of the enemy, it is not considered safe to fire our 9'2" Howitzers on 1st Lines, I consider they could be employed with great effect on enemy's 2nd line trenches.

STRONG POINTS. These will be known of beforehand and should be dealt with on days preceding the operations, care being taken to keep them under fire sufficient to prevent their being repaired.

Strong points encountered during attack and advance may be demolished by trench mortars carried forward with the attack especially for this purpose, otherwise a fresh bombardment must be
organised

organised on such points, if sufficiently strong to hold up the progress of the Infantry.

BARRAGE. I think much ammunition has been expended under this heading with inadequate results.

A Barrage on every known trench in the vicinity of operations unless movement is seen serves no useful purpose. I venture to think a more profitable procedure would be to have such trenches kept under close observation by forward observing officers, with orders to fire if movement is suspected or seen. At night Supplies, Reinforcements Etc., must be pushed forward, therefore after dark I suggest that all Cross Roads and suspected lines of advance be subjected to fairly frequent short sharp bursts of fire.

DURATION OF BOMBARDMENT. A preparation spread over a certain period followed by a sudden attack is the most likely to meet with success. The element of surprise should, as far as possible, be sought after, and possibly may be obtained by firing a series of short sharp bombardments with marked intervals in between. Such procedure may deceive the enemy as to when the assault is actually going to take place and may cause him to fill his trenches in the intervals between bombardments, more especially if our Infantry feint to attack when those bombardments cease. Care should be taken to prevent the bombardment ceasing suddenly before the real assault is launched, as this is not only dispiriting to our own Infantry, but also serves as a warning to the enemy to man his trenches, and permits of his recovering his morale. As previously stated I am strongly of opinion that the assault should not be ordered until the enemy's works are reported to be sufficiently demolished. ~~The template for the assault will thus be given from the front~~.

AMMUNITION. Against trenches and buildings generally H.E. is the most effective, as above appear to be the most common type of objective in the present phase of this war I recommend that H.E. for 18 pr. should be increased to at least 50%.

OBSERVATION POSTS. Must of necessity be located near our trenches. I should like, if possible, to see them controlled under some system. I suggest they should be arranged along the whole front a Division is covering, and that they should be sand bagged and made as safe as possible under the expert advice of the Engineers (this has been done with good results in the MEERUT Division).

Owing to frequent changes of front on the line it is difficult to put forward a suggestion to meet above proposal, but to illustrate the necessity of having Observation Posts properly established in all Divisions on our front, I bring the following to notice. It is not uncommon when a change of front on the line has been ordered, that a Battery Commander finds his new Observation Post insecure and a poor exchange for his last one, which he had taken the trouble to sandbag up and make reasonably safe. This in my opinion would not occur if all Observation Posts were controlled under a proper system on the fronts of Divisions.

A captive balloon (not spherical) should be employed to supplement aeroplane observation. There is no doubt that the recent increase of German "Sausage" Balloons has largely improved the fire effect of the German batteries.

CO-OPERATION WITH INFANTRY. Successful co-operation by Artillery means effective observation.

The system in vogue for co-operating with the Infantry when in the defence of the line works well and I think meets requirements at night provided the telephone is in working order, but if it is broken the following should be taken as signals for the battery to open fire on its "Night Lines":-

    (a) Rocket Signal from direction of front covered by the Battery.
    (b) Sudden heavy burst of rifle fire from same direction.

In offensive operations, Artillery Officers with telephone operators are detailed to accompany the Infantry, they report progress and establish new observing stations for directing Artillery fire

fire from, this system was employed with satisfactory results at NEUVE CHAPELLE.

COMMUNICATIONS. Obviously the more lines the better. A line of "heavy cable" per Artillery Brigade about a mile long, laid back from the neighbourhood of the principal Brigade Observation Posts buried in the ground is a useful safeguard in case overhead wires get cut an "exchange" being established at the end of this wire, which connects the batteries. Heavy Cable being the only relibale type of wire which can remain under ground for any length of time.

Lamps, visual signalling Etc, are also used and ready in case other communications fail.

RETALIATION. I am very strongly of opinion that when the enemy shell our trenches, that we should at once shell theirs in retaliation. (This procedure is followed when ammunition limits curtail the operations of the "Counter Batteries".) The system in vogue being, on our trenches being shelled, our batteries at once fire a few salvos on theirs. Generally speaking I think this plan answers the purpose and causes the enemy to stop shelling. At first this proceedure did not find favour with all sections on our line, but latterly the general opinion is that the method employed is satisfactory and produces the desired effect.

                    I have the honour to be,

                          Sir,

                    Your obedient servant,

                              Brigadier General R.A.

            Commanding Royal Artillery, MEERUT Division.

SECRET.

APPENDIX 252

TACTICAL PROGRESS REPORT
11th June 1915.

1.(a) ACTION BY OUR OWN ARTILLERY.

Observation of fire very difficult to-day owing to mist.
12.30.p.m. 8th Battery fired into a tree near R.10, suspected as snipers or observation post- the branches apparently being arranged for such purpose.
2.45.p.m. 2nd Battery checked registration of trench near R.8.
3.p.m. 8th Battery registered trench near V.3. where germans seen working.
3.30.p.m. 2nd Battery fired a few rounds at a german working party seen near R.8. This was repeated at 4.p.m.
4.30.p.m. 2nd Battery fired on germans crossing the fields beyond Q.16.
Batteries of 4th Brigade R.F.A. fired on enemy trenches in retaliation at intervals during the day.

(b) ACTION BY HOSTILE ARTILLERY.

4.a.m. to 5.a.m. 10.5.c.m. Howitzer shelled trenches of BAREILLY Bde.
9.20.a.m. PIPSQUEAK shelled front trenches from direction of LORGIES, and a few crumps were put in near RITZ from direction of BOIS du BIEZ.
10.30.a.m. PIPSQUEAK and WOOLY BEARS (10.5.c.m. how) shelled trenches in vicinity P.4 - P.5. from direction of VIOLAINES.
About 12 noon. German 105 mm howitzer shelled various parts of our trenches.
1.p.m. to 3.p.m. PIPSQUEAK shelled communication trench to V.1. and fire trench at intervals.
2.15.p.m. WOOLY BEARS shelled INDIAN VILLAGE (S 20 b.d.).
About 3.p.m. PIPSQUEAKS retaliated several times in a lively manner whilst 8th Battery were registering V.3.
3.30.p.m. to 4.15.p.m. 10.5.c.m. howitzer shelled M 27 d.
4.p.m. PIPSQUEAK put a few shell into LA COUTURE.

4.p.m. 10.5.c.m. howitzer shelled 19th Battery (S 7 b 1'6) for 20 mins.
4.15.p.m. 10.5.c.m. howitzer from direction LORGIES-appeared very close-shelled LA COUTURE also KING's Road.
4.20.p.m. PIPSQUEAK shelled INDIAN VILLAGE.
4.30.p.m. WOOLY BEARS shelled INDIAN VILLAGE fairly heavily for about 40 minutes.
5.10.p.m. Same battery switched on to Reserve trenches S 15 c for about 15 minutes.

2. INFORMATION.
MOVEMENTS:- Throughout the day germans were seen round about Q.15 and Q.16. At times they walked across the open from a heavily sand-bagged house near P.18 (about S 22 a 8'8) to a communication trench at Q.15. Communication trenches are being dug in this locality.
PIGEONS:- 11.45.a.m. Pigeon circled round LA COUTURE Church then made off in direction of LA BASSEE.
SEARCHLIGHTS:- Observed from M 32 a 4'5 on true bearings of 121°, 131°, 74° and 83°.
SUPPOSED O.P's:- Tree near R.10.
DOLL's House S 23 c 9'8 against which some planks have now been placed, and rounded clump of trees with ladder just N. of it.

R.K. Lynch-Staunton.
Major R.A.

Brigade Major, Royal Artillery,
MEERUT DIVISION.

FOLLOWING REPORT FROM 4th BRIGADE R.G.A. OPERATING ON MEERUT DIVISION FRONT:-

6.40.p.m. 10th June 1915:- 48th Heavy Battery engaged and quieted a howitzer firing on RUE du BOIS from S 30 central.
11th June 1915:-
9.15.a.m. Howitzer behind house at A 6 a 7'7(otherwise known as the cannon in residence) active and engaged and silenced pro-tem as usual.
10.5.a.m. A 4'2" howitzer shelling our trenches from VIOLAINES way S 30 central again engaged.
11.40.a.m. The "Cannon" again active and quieted.
11.50.a.m. T 19 a 3'1 believed active and engaged by Canadians.
1.p.m. S 24 b 0'10 engaged by 48th Heavy Battery and H.B.C.
1.30.p.m. S 24 a 10'10 engaged by Canadians and reported silenced.
3.10.p.m. Trench N. of H.7. reported shelled by howitzers from VIOLAINES and 48th Heavy Battery engaged A 6 a 7'7.
4.30.p.m. Howitzer active towards LA COUTURE not located so shelled LORGIES as counter irritant.
4.p.m. to 5.15.p.m. Trouble at times with BEAU PUITS and VIOLAINES batteries, both rather active.

SECRET.

APPENDIX 253

TACTICAL PROGRESS REPORT
12th June 1915.

1(a) ACTION BY OUR OWN ARTILLERY.

8.35.a.m. 66th Battery fired a few rounds at enemy's trenches in retaliation to enemy shelling ours.
11.15.a.m. 8th Battery fired in retaliation.
12.35.p.m. 14th Battery fired on trench 100 yards S.W. of P.14- explosion in trench one second later shell burst-likely bombs exploding.
12.45.p.m. 8th Battery registered points near DOLL's HOUSE.
12.57.p.m.,3.30.p.m. and 5.30.p.m. 2nd Battery fired at probable O.P. in tree near Q.15.
2.55.p.m. 2nd Battery fired in retaliation.
4.p.m. 66th Battery fired a few rounds at house near P.16 where three HUNS were seen to enter.
4.p.m. 8th Battery fired salvos in conjunction with MOTHER.
4.30.p.m. 44th Battery fired a few rounds on communication trenches S.E. of P.18 and registered a point on QUINQUE RUE.
4.45.p.m. 8th Battery fired a few rounds at tree near R.13- supposed O.P.
5.35.p.m. 2nd Battery registered on ridge S.W. of Q.15.
6.10.p.m. 2nd Battery fired at German waving flag in trench in S. part of FERME du BOIS.

(b) ACTION BY HOSTILE ARTILLERY.

During the morning 15.c.m. howitzer shelled our support trenches in vicinity of P.1. intermittently, and PIPSQUEAK did the same about N.9.
PIPSQUEAKS fired on our trenches intermittently all day- about 50% of the shell were blind.
7.50.a.m. 15.c.m. howitzer shelled INDIAN VILLAGE(S 20 a).
8.30.a.m. WOOLY BEARS shelled vicinity S 19 b (8 rounds)
9.10.a.m. PIPSQUEAK shelled 14th Battery O.P.(14 b 8'7 1/10,000 map).
9.30.a.m. 10.5.c.m. howitzer fired on our trenches near R.3.
9.45 to 10.a.m. 15.c.m. howitzer shelled vicinity S 14 a (a field just N. of RUE du BOIS)- nearly all were blind owing to soft ground, but detonated well on the road.
10.30.a.m. 15.c.m. howitzer shelled support trenches at N.12- 4 rounds battery fire one second- intervals good-range too short.
1.45.p.m. 15.c.m. howitzer fired on our communication trench near FACTORY causing some casualties.
2.p.m. 15.c.m. howitzer fired on EDWARD Road.
3.p.m. 15.c.m. howitzer shelled our support trenches in rear of V.2. from direction of LORGIES.
Two 15.c.m. shell fell near 14th Battery position- one blind.
3.15.p.m. PIPSQUEAK shelled 19th Battery position (S 7 b 1'8).
4.50.p.m. PIPSQUEAK shelled our Reserve trenches in front of INDIAN VILLAGE from direction of LORGIES. PIPSQUEAK again active at 5.15.p.m.
5.30.p.m. PIPSQUEAK shelled vicinity of X 18 b.

2. INFORMATION.
AIRCRAFT:- 11.15.a.m. SAUSAGE Balloon up true bearing due East from 66th Battery O.P.(9 c 5'0 1/10,000 map).
2.p.m. SAUSAGE over BEAU PUITS observing howitzer fire.
5.p.m. and 5.25.p.m. Hostile aeroplane over 66th and 14th Batteries came from direction of AUBERS.
7.p.m. German aeroplane flying over NEUVE CHAPELLE in N.E. direction.
MACHINE GUNS:- HIGHLAND Infantry in trenches near N.13 report Machine Gun located N.E. of N.13 on side of stream next LA QUINQUE RUE.

R.H. Lynch-Staunton, Major R.A.
Brigade Major, Royal Artillery,
MEERUT DIVISION.

P.T.O.

FOLLOWING REPORT FROM 1st BRIGADE R.G.A. OPERATING ON MEERUT DIVISION FRONT:-

4.20.p.m. No.1, 10th Siege Battery fired five rounds at the O.P.-DOLL's HOUSE:-
    2nd round struck the Right edge.
    4th round struck the top left hand corner.
    5th round struck the front of the house and brought it down.

FOLLOWING REPORT FROM 4th BRIGADE R.G.A. OPERATING ON MEERUT DIVISION FRONT:-

9.10.a.m. 48th Battery engaged T 8 d 7'8 as heavy crump gun active on ROUGE CROIX.
9.30.a.m. A few rounds at A 6 a 7'7 who went to ground.
10.a.m. Flashes seen 3° left of LA BASSEE from "PALACE" and stopped by 48th who placed guns at S 29 a 8'1.
11.a.m. T 19 c 4'7 active and engaged by 48th.
11.20.a.m. "SAUSAGE" up 5° right of ILLIES from "PALACE".
11.25.a.m. Engaged S 29 a 8'1 again.
1.20.p.m. Trenches in S 15 shelled by A 6 a 7'7 which was engaged and soon stopped.
1.59.p.m. S 30 central active in RUE du BOIS and engaged also the "Canon in Residence"(A 6 a 7'7) and both silenced.

SECRET.

APPENDIX 254

TACTICAL PROGRESS REPORT
13th June 1915.

1(a) ACTION BY OUR OWN ARTILLERY.
6.50.a.m. 66th Battery fired at trenches near Q.12 in reply to Huns shelling our Reserve trenches.
8.45.a.m. 8th Battery fired a few rounds at Germans seen working near Q.15.
10.30.a.m. 8th Battery fired registering rounds at Q.8 and Q.9.
11.30.a.m. 2nd Battery fired a few rounds on Q.15 to check registration.
3.40.p.m. 44th Battery fired on FERME COUR d'AVOINE in retaliation.
4.p.m. 14th Battery fired on M.12 and M.14 in retaliation to PIPSQUEAKS firing on our trenches.

(b) ACTION BY HOSTILE ARTILLERY.
10.p.m. 12th June 1915. 15.c.m. howitzer and PIPSQUEAK shelled our support trenches.
13th June 1915:-
8.30.a.m. Heavy howitzer shelled position lately vacated by 7th Battery just S. of RICHEBOURG.
8.30.a.m. 15.c.m. howitzer shelled INDIAN VILLAGE(S 20 b.d.).
9.15.a.m. WOOLY BEARS shelled vicinity of INDIAN VILLAGE from direction just N. of LA BASSEE.
10.5.a.m. Heavy howitzer shelled old and reserve trenches S.E. of RUE du BOIS.
10.a.m. 15.c.m. howitzer shelled vicinity of Q.7.
10.30.a.m. Heavy howitzer shelled PRINCES Road-thought to be registering KING's Road to DEAD COW FARM, aeroplane to S.E. seen to be observing for this battery.
10.35.a.m. 15.c.m. howitzer shelled X Road RUE de l'EPINETTE-RUE du BOIS.
12.15.p.m. 15.c.m. howitzer shelled BREWERY(S 20 c) for half an hour.
12.25.p.m. 15.c.m.(10.5 ?) howitzer shelled vicinity X 18 c for over an hour at odd intervals.
3.45.p.m.) WOOLY BEARS shelled RUE de l'EPINETTE(S 14 d) at 3.45.p.m.
4.p.m.   ) joined by PIPSQUEAKS at 4.p.m. firing salvos and later at
4.30.p.m.) 4.30.p.m. 15.c.m. howitzer at X Road X 18 c and vicinity
              until 5.15.p.m.
4.45.p.m. WOOLY BEARS shelled track from INDIAN VILLAGE to RUE de l'EPINETTE.
6.50.p.m. 15.c.m. howitzer and PIPSQUEAK shelled vicinity of RUE des BERCEAUX.
6.30.p.m. to 7.15.p.m. Area X.17 and X.18 and vicinity bombarded by PIPSQUEAK and 10.5.c.m. howitzer in retaliation to shelling of enemy's wire by HIGHLAND Divisional Artillery.

2. INFORMATION.
AIRCRAFT:- 7.57.a.m. 2nd Battery reported two german aeroplanes observing over trenches.
8.15.a.m. "SAUSAGE" Balloon up behind LORGIES.
8.40.a.m. 14th Battery report German aeroplane over battery(RICHEBOURG) flying in South Easterly direction.
9.a.m. 66th Battery reported two aeroplanes up in front of battery position(S.E. of RICHEBOURG), apparently observing- dropping lights.
9.10.a.m. German bi-plane flying over 44th Battery(M 32 d), was fired at by our Anti Aircraft Guns and retured in an Easterly direction throwing our three white lights at regular intervals.
10.25.a.m. 14th Battery reported german aeroplane flying over the trenches near the RITZ- retired on being fired at.
12.30.p.m. German "SAUSAGE" up bearing 158° from S 14 d 8'0.
4.6.p.m. Aeroplane observed coming from South dropping white signals. This machine became invisible presumably owing to clouds.
WIRE:- 7th Battery report that the enemy have strengthened the wire on their trench N.15 to 100 yards South of N14 during past night. This section of their trench is now strongly wired. The wire is laid in below-"Hallow" method.
New wire is visible along the hedge and fastened to trees N. of Q.15.
TRENCHES:- German communicating trench near R.10 has been deepened and overhead cover has been added at one or two points along it.

P.T.O.

TRENCHES(continued):- It is thought probable that the new trench reported to run along ditch N. of L.9 is not a fire trench, but that the germans may have boarded the natural ditch with planks and use it to go into when their trench is being shelled.
TRENCH MORTAR:- Reported by Infantry of "A" Sub-section at M.10 or just East of M.10.
REDOUBT:- Small square redoubt(about 9 feet square) located East of M.15 where german trench crosses the ditch which runs North and South between P.18 and M.13. It has good head cover and is loop-holed.
PROBABLE OBSERVATION POST:- The sand-bagged house S.E. of P.18 was fired at three times during the day when PIPSQUEAK and Howitzers shelled our trenches. Fire ceased immediately our guns opened fire on it, although our "retaliation" on their trenches on these occasions was ignored. This house is probably worthy of the gentle attentions of "MOTHER".

R K Lynch-Staunton.
Major R.A.

Brigade Major, Royal Artillery,
MEERUT DIVISION.

FOLLOWING REPORT FROM 4th BRIGADE R.G.A. OPERATING ON MEERUT DIVISION FRONT:-

3.20.a.m. 48th Heavy Battery opened fire on T 19 c 9'4 and T 19 d 9'9 searching and sweeping, because batteries at VIOLAINES and LORGIES were shelling our trenches.
5.35.a.m. Engaged the "Canon in Residence" A 6 a 7'7.
9.45.a.m. Fired at S 33 c 9'1 and S 30 central which batteries were both active.
12.10.p.m. A few rounds at T 1 a 9'9.
1.45.p.m. The "Canon" again active- stopped on being engaged.
2.50.p.m. Silenced S 30 central which was shelling the RUE du BOIS.
3.12.p.m. S 30 central opened fire again, but was stopped with two rounds.
3.40.p.m. Silenced battery at S 29 b 7'3.

A.E.W.

APPENDIX 255

S E C R E T.

TACTICAL PROGRESS REPORT
14th June 1915.

1(a) ACTION BY OUR OWN ARTILLERY.

7.20.p.m. 13th June 1915. 14th Battery fired a few rounds in retaliation to germans firing at our trenches.
14th June 1915.
4.15.a.m. 2nd Battery fired on german working party seen digging at Q.16. The party made off, but re-appeared and was again fired at at 5.15.a.m.- it then stopped work.
8.a.m. 44th Battery shelled position near M.14 where PIPSQUEAK flashes were seen.
44th Battery fired 10 rounds at O.P. near Q.15 at request of Infantry.
12 noon. 8th Battery registered trench Q.17 to P.19 with view to co-operation with 4th Corps.
2.50.p.m. 2nd Battery registered P.18 and Q.12 with view to co-operation with 4th Corps.
14th Battery fired a few rounds at intervals in retaliation for germans shelling our trenches.
5.50.p.m. 89th Battery fired 4 rounds at enemy's working party S.E. of L.17- fire effective.

(b) ACTION BY HOSTILE ARTILLERY.
German guns very quiet during the whole day.
7.45.a.m. 15.c.m. howitzer shelled RUE de l'EPINETTE.
9.15.a.m. Enemy howitzer(probably 15.c.m.)shelled 7th Battery O.P. Orchard(S 21 a) from direction of LA BASSEE.
9.25.a.m. 15.c.m. howitzer shelled support trenches in front of INDIAN VILLAGE(S 20 b.d.) from direction of LORGIES.
9.50.a.m. WOOLY BEARS shelled vicinity of S 13 b.
12 noon. PIPSQUEAK active on our front trenches and communication trench near V.1.
1.p.m. to 2.p.m. 10.5.c.m. howitzer shelled REVOLVER HOUSE(S 3 a) and S 2 d.
1.30.p.m. Light howitzer and PIPSQUEAK shelled road between WINDY CORNER and St. VAAST.
2.30.p.m. WOOLY BEARS shelled track from INDIAN VILLAGE to RUE de l'EPINETTE for half an hour.

2. INFORMATION.
Much less movement to-day round the FERME du BOIS.
HOSTILE BATTERIES:- PIPSQUEAK Battery reported either about S 28 d 5'7 or else in Orchard N. of house S 28 b 3'6 known as M.14 on trench map(References-BETHUNE Combined Sheet 1/40,000 2nd Ed.
TRENCH MORTARS:- 8.20.a.m. Enemy's trench mortar fired on "A" Sub-section support trenches- all blind.
TRENCHES:- 7th Battery report trench running from Cross Roads A 4 c 4'4 N.W. to J.20 where it is hidden by a hedge. Trench appears unoccupied and no wire visible. It may be a communication trench leading to trench East of RUE d'OUVERT.
FIRES:- 10.38.a.m. LARGE fire at VIOLAINES.

R.K. Lynch-Staunton.

Major R.A.

Brigade Major, Royal Artillery,
MEERUT DIVISION.

FOLLOWING REPORT FROM 4th BRIGADE R.G.A. OPERATING ON MEERUT DIVISION FRONT:-

48th Heavy Battery:-

9.50.a.m. Engaged single howitzers at N 32 c 1'3 and T 20 b 3'1.
10.30.a.m. Fired at a house in N 32 c 1'3 setting it on fire. After about $\frac{3}{4}$ of an hour, thick black smoke poured out, which was possible some kind of stores burning.
10.55.a.m. Engaged S 6 b 3'0.
11.45.a.m. Engaged S 6 b 3'0 again.
12 noon. Engaged S 24 b 0'10.
12.55.p.m. Fired at T 1 a 3'7.
1.30.p.m. Engaged T.14 a 0'0 and then T 14 c 0'0.
1.50.p.m. Located battery T 14 c 9'8 which was shelling behind the TROC- engaged it.
6.15.p.m. Engaged the "Canon in Residence"-A 6 a 7'7.
3.20.p.m. Fired at S 23 c 9'1.

1st BRIGADE R.G.A. WORKING IN CO-OPERATION WITH THE 4th CORPS.

Copy No. 4

Extract from Indian Corps Operation Order No.71 of 11/6/15.

APPENDIX 256

SECRET

1. The 4th Corps is resuming the offensive on the evening of the 14th June after a preliminary bombardment lasting 60 hours. The 51st (Highland) Division is being directed on the Northern end of RUE D'OUVERT, the 7th Division on the southern end and against CHAPELLE ST ROCH, while the Canadian Division forms a defensive flank I.17, I.16, N.2

2. During this period the Indian Corps will co-operate as follows:-
   (a) The 8th Division will act in accordance with special instructions already communicated.
   (b) The Lahore Division will carry out a minor operation on the evening of 14th June against the enemy line V.1 - V.2 - V.3, the details of which have been communicated separately.

15th

G 352

No G 339

      x   x   x

For information.

Copy No. 1 to Dehra Dun Bde
     2   Garhwal Bde
     3   Bareilly Bde
     4   C.R.A. Meerut
     5   C.R.E. Meerut
     6   4th Ind. Cavalry
     7   107th Pioneers
  8. to 12 War Diary & files.

Colonel,
General Staff,
MEERUT DIVISION.

APPENDIX 15

S E C R E T.

Extract from Indian Corps Operation Order No.71 dated 11th June 1915, received under cover of MEERUT Division No.G-239 dated the 11th June 1915.

1. The 4th Corps is resuming the offensive on the evening of the 15th June after a preliminary bombardment lasting 60 hours. The 51st (Highland) Division is being directed on the Northern end of RUE d' OUVERT, the 7th Division on the Southern end and against CHAPELLE St. ROCH, while the Canadian Division forms a defensive flank I.17, I.16, H.8.

2. During this period the Indian Corps will co-operate as follows:-
    (a) The 8th Division will act in accordance with special instructions already communicated.
    (b) The LAHORE Division will carry out a minor operation on the evening of the 15th June against the enemy line V.1.-V.2.-V.3, the details of which have been communicated separately.

No.788-R.A.(L).   Headquarters Divisional Artillery,
                                         MEERUT DIVISION.

                                         11th June 1915.

To,
    The Officers Commanding,
        4th Brigade R.F.A.   Copy No.1.
        9th Brigade R.F.A.   Copy No.2.
        13th Brigade R.F.A.   Copy No.3.
        MEERUT Divisional Ammunition Column. Copy No.4.

Forwarded for information.

                                                    Major R.A.
                                  Brigade Major, Royal Artillery,
                                      MEERUT DIVISION.

Copy No.5

APPENDIX 25

SECRET.

No. G.352
Headquarters, Meerut Division.
11th June 1915.

Corrigenda to Indian Corps Operation Order No.71 issued with my G.339 of date.

In paragraphs 1 and 2(b) for "14th June" read "15th June".

To,
Dehra Dun Bde
Garhwal Bde
Bareilly Bde
C.R.A.
C.R.E.
4th Ind.Cav.
107th Pioneers
A.A. & Q.M.G.

Major,
General Staff,
MEERUT DIVISION.

No 745- RA(L) APPENDIX 25

SECRET.

Headquarters Divisional Artillery,
MEERUT DIVISION.

12th June 1915.

To,
The Officers Commanding,
4th Brigade R.F.A.
9th Brigade R.F.A.
13th Brigade R.F.A.
MEERUT Divisional Ammunition Column.

The following correction is made to the Extract from INDIAN Corps Operation Order No.71 forwarded to you under my No. 732-R.A.(L) dated the 11th June 1915:-

In paragraphs 1 and 2(b) for "14th June" read "13th June".

Please acknowledge.

Major R.A.

Brigade Major, Royal Artillery,
MEERUT DIVISION.

SECRET.

APPENDIX 260

Headquarters, Meerut Division.
13th June 1915.

Copy of a memorandum from Indian Corps to Meerut Division No. G.773 dated 13/6/15.

Reference Indian Corps Operation Order No.71 dated 11th June 1915, please arrange to co-operate with the 4th Corps to the extent of bringing 18-pr shrapnel fire to bear on:-

(a) The communication trench P.19 to Q.17 near FME DE ~~GODOGON~~ TOULOTTE.

(b) The road P.18 - Q.12.

between the hours of 7.30 P.M. and ~~5 A.M.~~ 4.30 a.m. on the night of 14th/15th June, and also from 5.45 p.m. to ~~8.30~~ 9 p.m. on the ~~afternoon~~ evening of 15th June, or later on demand

2. An allowance of ~~120~~ 160 rounds should suffice for the above purpose. up to 9 p m on 15th June 1915

No. G.394.

C.R.A. MEERUT DIVN.

Forwarded for information and necessary action, reference my G.339 of 11th instant.

P. Davies, Major
~~Colonel,~~
General Staff,
Meerut Division.

Corrected vide Indian Corps G 786 14/6/15

"A" Form. Army Form C. 2121.

MESSAGES AND SIGNALS. No. of Message ....

APPX 261

Prefix .... Code .... m.	Words	Charge	This message is on a/c of:	Recd. at .... m.
Office of [illegible] and Service Instructions.			.... Service.	Date ....
	Sent			From ....
	At .... m.			
	To			
	By		(Signature of "Franking Officer.")	By ....

TO 15 [illegible] Bde

Sender's Number.	Day of Month.	In reply to Number	AAA
* KM 7[illegible]	13		

Tomorrow night our section will be prepared to barrage Road Q 12 [illegible] [illegible] the section [illegible] P 17 to Q 17 [illegible] [illegible] commence [illegible] [illegible] [illegible] [illegible]

From KMRA
Place
Time 1 [illegible] pm

The above may be forwarded as now corrected. **(Z)** [illegible]

Censor. Signature of Addressor or person authorised to telegraph in his name.

* This line should be erased if not required.

(B10111)—Wt. W 14142/641—2,000,000—3/15. S. & S., Ltd.

No. CRA 62.   SECRET   14th June 1915

O.C. 13th Brigade R.H.A.   APPX 262

In continuation of my BM 747 of yesterday's date, under instructions from INDIAN Corps, through MEERUT Division, please arrange to co-operate with the 4th Corps (vide my No 732 RA(a) 11.6.1915) by carrying out the following beginning:—

(a) Communication trench P.19 to Q.17
(b) Road P.18 to Q.12.

between the hours of 7.30 pm and 3 am on the night of 14th/15th June.

2. Four rounds shrapnel should be fired each half hour commencing 7.45 pm, this will allow of 30 bursts of 4 rounds each or total of 120 rounds being brought to bear on the two tasks during period mentioned.

3. From 5.45 pm to 6.16 pm on afternoon of 15th June tasks mentioned in 1(a) and 1(b) above will be repeated, an allowance of 15 shrapnel for each or total of 30.

4. During afternoon and evening 15th batteries should be on the look out to stop any movement from N. to S. in vicinity of Q.12 to P.14 or from Q.17 P.18 towards N.15

R.W. Lynch-Staunton Major RA
Brigade Major RA
Meerut Division

Copy to G.O.C GARHWAL Bde
for information

SECRET.

Meerut Division

APPx 263
14/6/15 (3 pages)

At the request of the 4th Corps my No. G-773 dated 13th June 1915 is modified as under:-

Erase from the words "between the hours ...." to the end of the letter, and substitute:-
"between the hours of 7.30 p.m. and 4.30 a.m. on the night of 14th/15th June and also from 5.45 p.m. to 9.0 p.m. on the evening of 15th June, or later on demand.

2. An allowance of 160 rounds should suffice for the above purpose up to 9.0 p.m. on 15th June."

Indian Corps.   General Staff.

G. 422
Headquarters, Meerut Division.
14th June 1915 - 2.40 P.M.

C.R.A. Meerut Division.

Forwarded for information in modification of my No. G. 394 of yesterday.

2. Please say if the allotment of rounds given appears to you to be sufficient.

Colonel,
General Staff,
Meerut Division.

No.749-R.A.(L).

Headquarters Divisional Artillery,
MEERUT DIVISION.

14th June 1915.

To,

The General Staff,
MEERUT DIVISION.

Your No.G-422 dated 14th June 1915 noted.

2. Allotment mentioned appears decidedly inadequate to achieve purpose, vide my No.746-R.A.(L) of date.

I have suggested that 8 rounds per task per hour is the minimum which can in any way be regarded as likely to effectively achieve the object in view.

I therefore suggest that 24 additional rounds are required for period 3.a.m. to 4.30.a.m. on the 15th.

For period 5.45.p.m. to 9.p.m. on same basis 56 rounds would now be required instead of 30 rounds previously sanctioned, giving an increase of 26 rounds for this period.

Total required would therefore be:-

    150 plus 24 plus 26 = 200 rounds.

I should like to point out that we are now called upon to shoot for an additional four hours and twenty minutes and have only been allotted ten extra rounds for this purpose.

J.H.MacFarlane
Lieut R.A.
for Brigadier General R.A.
Commanding Royal Artillery, MEERUT Division.

No. G. 425
Headquarters, Meerut Division.
14th June 1915 - 5.0 P.M.

C.R.A. Meerut Divn.

Reference your 749-R.A.L. of date.

Ammunition is sanctioned up to 216 rounds.

& Colonel,
General Staff,
Meerut Division.

C.R.A.63.   SECRET   APPENDIX 26
                              14th June 1915.   86

O.C. 13th Brigade R.H.A.

Cancel lines 8 to 19 of my C.R.A.62 of
today's date and ~~include~~ substitute the
following:-
"Between the hours of 7.30.p.m. and 4.30.a.m.
on the night of 14th/15th June.
2. Four rounds shrapnel should be fired
each half hour commencing 7.45.p.m.
3. From 5.45.p.m. to 9.p.m. on evening
of 15th June tasks mentioned in 1(a) and 1(b)
above will be repeated, four rounds shrapnel
being fired (vide para 2 above.
(every half hour.)
Total of ammunition expended
not to exceed 216 rounds."   J.H.M.Hulme
                                    Lieut R.A.
                              for Brigade Major R.A.
                                    Meerut Division.

Copy to:-
        G.O.C. Garhwal Bde for information

SECRET.

APPENDIX 265

TACTICAL PROGRESS REPORT
15th June 1915.

1(a) ACTION BY OUR OWN ARTILLERY.

7.45.p.m. 14.6.15.) 2nd and 8th Batteries carried out Barrages as
      to   ) ordered, to co-operate with IV Corps i,e,, P.19
4.30.a.m. 15.6.15.) to Q.17 and P.18 to Q.12, a few rounds every
              half hour.
During the night 14th/15th 36th Battery fired a few rounds on
enemy's working party near Q.11 at request from Infantry.
11.20.a.m. 2nd Battery engaged DISTILLERY as ordered by MEERUT
Division, on receipt of information from INDIAN Corps that several
motor cars were halted in road outside. Probably Staff observing
from there.
11.45.a.m. 14th and 66th Batteries fired a few rounds at German
trenches in retaliation to their shelling ours
12.30.p.m. 14th Battery fired at working party W. of P.14 at
request of Infantry.
3.20.p.m. 66th Battery shelled sand-bagged house S. of Q.12 in
retaliation to germans shelling our trenches N. of Q.7.
5.45.p.m. to 8.45.p.m. P.19 to Q.17 and P.18 to Q.12 were
barraged at slow rate to assist operations of IV Corps.
6.p.m. 8th Battery fired a few rounds in retaliation to germans
firing on trenches of "B" Sub-section.

(b) ACTION BY HOSTILE ARTILLERY.

11.15.a.m. PIPSQUEAKS shelled our support trenches.
1.20.p.m. Heavy howitzer shelled fire trench of "A" Sub-section.
3.35.p.m. to 4.p.m. 15.c.m. howitzer and PIPSQUEAK shelled CROIX
BARBEE and to N.W. of that point. About 50 shell. Ten casualties
near Cross Roads.
3.p.m. to 7.p.m. 15.c.m. and 10.5.c.m. howitzers shelled RUE du
BOIS and RUE des BERCEAUX.
9.20.p.m. Two heavy "crumps" fell in front of 14th Battery position
in S 2 c.
During the afternoon enemy shelled road N. of WINDY CORNER.

2. INFORMATION.

AIRCRAFT:- 8.20.a.m. Observation balloon seen ascending in Easterly
direction from 14th Battery.
11.5.a.m. German "SAUSAGE" up bearing $107\frac{1}{2}°$ from S 14 a 10'10.
11.50.a.m. Aeroplane over a point 500 yards S.(approx) of 44th
Battery, showed 3 white lights and then disappeared in S.W.
direction.
5.22.p.m. German aeroplane flying low over 10th Siege Battery(R.30)
LIGHTS:- 5.35.p.m. Germans sending out green lights and a red one
from the FERME du BOIS.
5.45.p.m. Germans sending our red lights from V.2.
PIGEONS:- 4.30.a.m. A covey of pigeons was seen flying across the
RUE du BOIS near LEICESTER LOUNGE in N.E. direction.

R.K. Lynch-Staunton.
                  Major R.A.

Brigade Major, Royal Artillery,
      MEERUT DIVISION.

P.T.O

FOLLOWING REPORT FROM 4th BRIGADE R.G.A.:-

109th Heavy Battery:-
12 noon registered DISTILLERY(S 17 central).
5.p.m. According to 4th Brigade orders engaged S 6 b 3'0-N 32 c 1'0-S 6 b 5'5-S 24 b 0'10.
5.45.p.m. Gun fire on S 24 b 0'10.
6.p.m. Gun fire on all four.
6.10.p.m. Fired at S 12 a 5'1 and FERME du BIEZ.
6.20.p.m. Engaged T 14 a 9'9 and T 15 d 1'4.
6.28.p.m. ceased fire.
6.45.p.m. Fired 7 rounds at T 20 a 10'9.

110th Heavy Battery:-
Registered battery in DISTILLERY, Ranging House and N.W. corner of the BOIS.
4.p.m. Engaged T 1 c 9'6 with aeroplane- results good.
5.p.m. to 6.30.p.m. Engaged S 11 d 3'3, S 17 b 4'3, S 12 c 6'3, S 12 b 5'0 S 18 a 4'2.
5.40.p.m. Shrapnel fire on PIPSQUEAK behind DISTILLERY- seemed effective.

48th Heavy Battery:-
9.30.a.m. Engaged A 6 a 7'7.
10.58.a.m. Engaged A 6 a 7'7 by flashes again.
11.40.a.m. Fired at S 23 c 9'1- registered T.S. and Lyd. range.
3.10.p.m. Engaged S 18 c 10.0 believed active on RUE du BOIS.
5.p.m. Engaged T 19 a 7'4- T 14 c 9'8- S 24 b 0'10.
5.28.p.m. Fired shrapnel at A 6 a 7'7.
5.42.p.m. Shelled S 29 b 8'8.
5.50.p.m. O.P. saw two green rockets up.
5.53.p.m. Aeroplane target A 12 d 5'5.
5.58.p.m. Engaged S 11 d 3'3.
6.15.p.m. Engaged aeroplane target T 19 d 3'5, also S 24 b 0'10.
7.40.p.m. Engaged by aeroplane T 20 b 4'4 and then S 29 b 2'3.

From 5.p.m. the batteries were firing in co-operation with the LAHORE Divisional Artillery.

"A" Form. Army Form C. 2121.

MESSAGES AND SIGNALS.

Prefix	Code	Words	Charge	*This message is on a/c of:	Recd. at 3/7 p.m.
SA	OP	57	APPX 265a	Service.	Date 16/3/15
9/15 Brock		Sent At ... m. To ... By ...		(Signature of "Franking Officer.")	From ... By ...

TO — C R A Meerut

Sender's Number	Day of Month	In reply to Number	AAA
G483	16th		

Indian corps wire G819 begins in confirmation telephonic instructions detail one 18 Pdr Bty of your Divn to carry out special task in operations 4th Corps AAA Details have been communicated by General SCOTT to CRH Meerut addressed Meerut Divn repeated 4th Corps ends AAA action

From
Place Meerut
Time 3.15

The above may be forwarded as now corrected. (Z)

"A" Form.　Army Form C. 2121.

MESSAGES AND SIGNALS.

Prefix... Code... m. | Words | Charge | This message is on a/c of... | Recd. at...
Office of Origin and Service Instructions. | | Sent At... m. | Service. | Date
by hand SECRET | | To... By... | (Signature of "Franking Officer.") | From... By...

APPENDIX 265 7

TO:
Dehra Dun Bde　CRA Meerut
Garhwal Bde　CRE Meerut "QA"
Bareilly Bde　Genl Anderson

Sender's Number: G 478　Day of Month: 16th　In reply to Number:　　AAA

Indian Corps wires begins G816 — 11.40 AM The fourth Corps is resuming its operations according to the same programme as yesterday but the assault is fixed for 4.45 p.m and all arrangements will be advanced seventyfive minutes AAA The Artillery of the Meerut Divn will cooperate in the same manner as yesterday ends Addressed CRA for necessary action AAA Acknowledge repeated Brigades and CRE for information

From: Meerut Divn
Place:
Time: 12.15 PM

The above may be forwarded as now corrected.　(Z)
Censor.　Signature of Addressor or person authorised to telegraph in his name.
* This line should be erased if not required.
(688-9) —McC. & Co. Ltd., London.— W 14142/641. 225,000. 4.15. Forms C 2121/10.

SECRET.

TACTICAL PROGRESS REPORT
13th June 1915.

APPENDIX 266

1(a) ACTION BY OUR OWN ARTILLERY.
2nd and 8th Batteries carried out firing during the night and to-day as ordered (Barrages P.18 to Q.12 and P.19 to Q.17) to co-operate with IV Corps.
11.a.m. 44th Battery fired at PIPSQUEAK whose flashes were observed in direction of M.25- fired up to 6,100 yards but failed to reach it.
2.20.p.m. Orders received from INDIAN Corps for one 18 pr. Battery to be placed at disposal of 9th Brigade R.F.A. for co-operation with IV Corps. 7th Battery was selected for this and task allotted.
2.35.p.m. 66th Battery fired at trenches S. of P.17 in retaliation for shelling of our reserve trenches by heavy howitzers.
3.18.p.m. 14th Battery fired a few rounds at trenches in retaliation.
7th Battery fired at German trench L.12 to 200 yards E.N.E. till 5.30.p.m. to co-operate with IV Corps(see 2.20.p.m.)
4.30.p.m. 2nd and 8th Batteries again formed barrages at slow rate until 7.30.p.m. to co-operate with IV Corps.
4.50.p.m. 14th Battery fired at O.P. M.12 in response to PIPSQUEAK shelling trenches.
6.p.m. 66th Battery fired on sand-bagged house S.E. of P.15 in retaliation for PIPSQUEAK firing on our reserve trenches.

(b) ACTION BY HOSTILE ARTILLERY.
8.45.p.m. to 11.15.p.m. 15.6.15. Heavy howitzer (21.c.m.) shelled a little short of 14th Battery from direction of ILLIES.
10.40.a.m. 15.c.m. howitzer shelled trenches near P.8. till 11.20.a.m. from direction of LORGIES. Again active at 3.30.p.m.
11.40.a.m. PIPSQUEAK at M.30 active. This requires attention of Heavy Artillery- out of range of our field guns.
Some PIPSQUEAKS fired on the RUE du BOIS during the day.

2. INFORMATION.
AIRCRAFT:- 7.45.a.m. 13th Brigade R.F.A. reported German aeroplane to the West.
9.15.a.m. Hostile aeroplane flying East of left flank of 14th Battery - reconnoitring.
9.40.a.m. Hostile aeroplane flying in Easterly direction away from 66th Battery.
3.10.p.m. Captive balloon observed true bearing 118° 35' from S 32 a 4'8. BAREDE.
7.5.p.m. Hostile aeroplane seen flying from East to West. near CROIX
PIGEONS:- 11.22.a.m. Covey of pigeons seen flying S.W. over RICHEBOURG.
1.40.p.m. One pigeon seen rising from ruins of FERME COUR d'AVOUE.
FLAGS:- The Red Cross flag has disappeared from LA BASSEE.
SIGNALLING:- 4.30.a.m. and 6.p.m. German seen signalling with flag near N.25.
IDENTIFICATION SCREENS:- 9th Brigade R.F.A.(attached IV Corps) reports that during to-day's operations the HUNS displayed the Identification Screens used by the HIGHLAND Division in the attack yesterday. Evidently with idea of deceiving our Artillery.
It so happened a different coloured screen had been adopted by this Division for to-day's operations !
MACHINE GUNS:- Located in house 20 yards N.W. of P.14.
BOMB GUNS:- 4 reported from same house and from trench 30 yards S.W. of it.
GERMAN PICQUET:- Frequent same house at night.

R.K. Lynch-Staunton,
Major R.A.

Brigade Major, Royal Artillery,
MEERUT DIVISION.

REPORT RECEIVED FROM 4th BRIGADE R.G.A. OPERATING ON MEERUT DIVISION FRONT:-
The batteries of the 4th Brigade R.G.A. did good and useful shooting during to-day's operations, engaging and silencing many batteries. The 109th Heavy Battery made the German "SAUSAGE" descend twice during the day, the first time after the third round.

SECRET.

APPENDIX 267

TACTICAL PROGRESS REPORT
17th June 1915.

(a) ACTION BY OUR OWN ARTILLERY.
Batteries of the 4th Brigade R.F.A. fired a few rounds in retaliation to germans shelling our trenches.
12.30.p.m. 8th Battery registered new line of trench marked out with stakes between FERME du BOIS and R.9.
4.15.p.m. 14th Battery fired a few rounds in conjunction with 48th Heavy Battery shelling P.14. 2nd Battery assisted 48th Heavy Battery with observation. 48th Heavy Battery scored several direct hits on ruin of which only portions of walls existed before. Heavy howitzer fire required to "do in" the cellars

(b) ACTION BY HOSTILE ARTILLERY.
PIPSQUEAK fired a few rounds at our communication trenches during the morning.
7.50.a.m. WOOLY BEARS shelled vicinity S.W. of BREWERY (S 20 c) from direction of VIOLAINES.
9.20.a.m. 15.c.m. howitzer shelled vicinity of S 19 c.
Between 10.a.m. and 11.a.m. Some 10.5.c.m. and PIPSQUEAK fell near CROIX BARBEE.
11.a.m. to 12 noon. 10.5.c.m. howitzer fired on CROIX BAREEE direction, and also on line through recent position of 44th Battery towards the 48th Heavy Battery.
11.5.a.m. 15.c.m. howitzer and PIPSQUEAK shelled support trenches in front of INDIAN VILLAGE.
11.30.a.m. Six 10.5.c.m. shell fell near position lately occupied by the 44th Battery.
11.50.a.m. One shell fell within four yards of Headquarters of 4th Brigade R.F.A. wounding two gunners.
3.p.m. 15.c.m. howitzer shelled house S 25 b 5'7 (3 direct hits) and reserve trenches in front of INDIAN VILLAGE.
3.30.p.m. 21.c.m. howitzer shelled Reserve trenches in front of FESTUBERT, also front line trench near QUINQUE RUE.
6.p.m. 10.5.c.m. howitzer fired towards DOLL's HOUSE M 27 d 7'4.

2. INFORMATION.
TRENCHES:- Trench from S.E. corner of FERME du BOIS towards R.9. has been improved and wire on low stakes placed in front during last two nights.
Much work has been done on communication trenches S., S.W. and N.W. of R.9.
Trench between R.8. and V.2. much strengthened and fresh communication trenches sand-bagged immediately in rear.
Intermittent work was in progress here to-day.
Fresh works have been constructed about 100 yards N.E. of R.10.
AIRCRAFT:- 5.7.a.m. Hostile bi-plane travelling E. to W., returning to E. on left of 44th Battery.
7.18.a.m. Hostile bi-plane seen in vicinity of CROIX BARBEE- dropped two white lights. Was engaged by Archibalds.
7.25.a.m. Hostile bi-plane observed travelling in Northernly direction.
7.40.a.m. Hostile aeroplane appeared from S. flying off to E.
9.24.a.m. Hostile plane seen flying S. over trenches reconnoitring S. of RICHEBOURG.
2.40.p.m. Two captive balloons observed from M 32 a 0'8 at true bearings 119° and 198°.
5.25.p.m. Hostile plane reconnoitring over RUE du BOIS and CROIX BARBEE; was engaged by our Archibalds.
6.32.p.m. Hostile aeroplane flying S. of trenches then East.

R.M. Lynch-Hunter, Major R.A.
Brigade Major, Royal Artillery,
MEERUT DIVISION.

P.T.O.

ACTION BY 1st BRIGADE R.G.A. OPERATING ON OUR FRONT:-

MOTHER engaged in registering RUE d'OUVERT.
8th Siege Battery engaged hostile batteries at A 6 d 8'4, A 6 a 7'7 and T 16 a 7'7.

ACTION BY 4th BRIGADE R.G.A. OPERATING ON OUR FRONT:-

48th Heavy Battery engaged T 4 c 2'5, S 29 a 9'1, A 6 a 7'7, T 20 b 4'4, T 5 c 9'7 during the day.
109th Heavy Battery engaged howitzer T 19 a 2'2.
110th Heavy Battery engaged PIPSQUEAK at S 17 b 3'3.

"A" Form. Army Form C. 2121.
MESSAGES AND SIGNALS.

SECRET.

APPENDIX 267a

TO: Dehra Dun Bde   Garhwal Bde   Bareilly Bde
C.R.A. Meerut   C.R.E. Meerut

Sender's Number.	Day of Month	In reply to Number	
G.527	18th		AAA

Following from Indian Corps for information reference my G.517 of yesterday AAA Begins AAA Operations of IVth Corps arranged to take place early this morning have been postponed 24 hours from time originally fixed AAA acknowledge ends Addressed Brigades C.R.E. repeated C.R.A. for information

From: Meerut Div
Time: 8.0 A.M.

Col.

"A" Form. Army Form C. 2121.

MESSAGES AND SIGNALS.

Prefix	Code	Words	Charge	This message is on a/c of:	Recd. at ... m.

SECRET (by hand)

APPENDIX Date 26/7

Service. From

(Signature of "Franking Officer.") By

TO — O.C. 4th Bde R.F.A.
O.C. 13th Bde R.F.A.

Sender's Number	Day of Month	In reply to Number	AAA
BM812	18		AAA

Following from MEERUT DIVN for information begins following from Indian Corps for information reference my G(S17) of yesterday AAA Begins AAA Operations of IVth Corps arranged to take place early this morning have been postponed 24 hours from time originally fixed AAA Acknowledge ends Addressed Brigades CRE repeated CRA for information AAA ends acknowledge

From Meerut DIV ARTY
Place
Time 9-49 a.m.

The above may be forwarded as now corrected. (Z)

Censor. Signature of Addressor or person authorised to telegraph in his name.

*This line should be erased if not required.

SECRET.

APPENDIX 268

TACTICAL PROGRESS REPORT
18th June 1915.

1(a) ACTION BY OUR OWN ARTILLERY.
7.15.a.m. 2nd Battery fired 6 rounds on DISTILLERY owing to German field guns shelling RUE du BOIS.
7.42.a.m. 14th Battery fired at R.12 - registration for IV Corps operations.
8.30.a.m. 66th Battery fired at sand-bagged house S.E. of P.17 in conjunction with 48th Heavy Battery, which obtained 3 direct hits
11.a.m. 8th Battery fired at germans working in their trench between R.8. and Q.15.
11.30.a.m. 44th Battery fired 12 rounds at a farm near P.18
11.45.a.m. 14th Battery registered X.14, X.18, X.19 and X.20 - task for co-operation with IV Corps.
1.47.p.m. 66th Battery fired at sand-bagged house S.E. of P.17 in reply to enemy shelling our trenches.
1.50.p.m. 2nd Battery engaged DISTILLERY getting some nice hits; but this did not stop fire of heavy howitzers on Leicesters trenches.
3.10.p.m. 2nd Battery registered points for co-operation with IV Corps.
4.30.p.m. and 5.25.p.m. 8th Battery fired on working party in trench near R.10.
6.15.p.m. 14th Battery fired at working party 70 yards S.W. of P.1
7.45.p.m. Section 55th Howitzer Battery registered Q.15 and P.14.

(b) ACTION BY HOSTILE ARTILLERY.
77.mm. shelled communication trenches of HIGHLAND Division a good deal during the night, and Reserve trenches S. of INDIAN VILLAGE. Very little hostile field gun shelling to-day.
4.40.a.m. 77.mm. shelled trenches round M.9 very heavily.
8.30.a.m. 15.c.m. howitzer shelled support trenches L.5 - L.7.
11.a.m. to 12 noon. Heavy howitzers fired short of 48th Heavy Battery dropping shells about M 31 b.
12 noon. 15.c.m. howitzer shelled FESTUBERT.
1.20.p.m. 15.c.m. howitzer shelled vicinity X 19 c, S 19 b for an hour in bursts of 2 and 4 rounds.
1.30.p.m. to 2.30.p.m. Heavy howitzers fired on area S.W. of RICHEBOURG.(believed to be 21.c.m.).
1.50.p.m. Leicester's trenches heavily shelled by heavy howitzers- 2nd Battery retaliated on DISTILLERY.
3.45.p.m. 21.c.m.(15.c.m.?) shelled INDIAN VILLAGE.
5.10.p.m. to 7.10.p.m. 21.c.m. howitzer believed to be at WARNETON (T 10 c 2'3) was firing on RUE des BERCEAUX with wireless aeroplane observation. Aeroplane gave 2 "Targets" and O.K. on old HIGHLAND Artillery position before flying home last time.

2. INFORMATION.
AIRCRAFT:- 12 noon. Captive balloon observed at 119° from M 32 a 0'8.
5.25.p.m. to 6.45.p.m.(7.p.m.?) German bi-plane with "wireless" observing for 21 c.m. howitzer at WARNETON, which was firing on S 8 a 3'0. Appeared undisturbed or out of range of our Anti Aircraft Guns, and the "fighting" plane did not appear to spot it.
TRENCHES:- Work done during the night on new trench FERME du BOIS to R.9.

Lynch-Staunton, Major R.A.

Brigade Major, Royal Artillery,
MEERUT DIVISION.

P. T. O.

4th BRIGADE R.G.A. OPERATING ON OUR FRONT REPORT AS FOLLOWS:-

Engaged following during day;-
S 35 d 1.0, A 6 a 7.7, T 21 b 3.4, T 10 a 0.6, S 19 a 5.1,
S 34 b 0.10, T 15 a 5.6, T 20 c.8.8, T 14 c 9.8, T 31 b 3.5,
T 20 b 4.2, T 15 c 5.0, S 13 c 5.5, S 20 b 5.2, T 20 a 5.1,
A 6 b 8.0 and LORGIES, also fired on hostile activity seen at
S 35 c, T 10 c, A 3 a during the morning.

SECRET.

Meerut D A
APPENDIX 268a

4th CORPS & ATTACHED ARTILLERY

INSTRUCTIONS No.8

1. With the object of deceiving the enemy and pinning him to his present positions, the 4th Corps will make pretence of attacking the line L.13 – K.7, on the morning of the 19th inst:

2. At 3.40 am small detachments of infantry will move forward out of their trenches near the salient L.8 and in the neighbourhood of H.2, H.3 and lie down in the grass as if in preparation to assault the enemy's positions.

3. 3.30 – 3.40 the artillery will commence a bombardment of the enemy's trenches with 18 pdrs.
   3.40 – 3.43am PAUSE – STOP FIRING.
   3.43 – 4am the bombardment will be continued; batteries will search backwards and forwards with Shrapnel for ~~200~~ 350 yds during the first 10 minutes after the pause, continuing with H.E. till 4 am
   4 am CEASE FIRING.

   The following tasks are allotted:–
   Canadian Div: Arty.   – H.8 – bend W of H.4
   18 pdr Batteries   L.3 – L.9 – L.13 – J.14.

   Alexander Group.
      22nd Brigade   – Main trench W of J.13 – K.7.
      French Brigade   – Trench J.10-K.3.

   Nicholson Group.   – Z. inclusive – K.3
                            Main trench K.7 – L.10.

   Highland Div. Art. –
      8th Bde R.F.A.   – Main trench L.10 – Z.3.
      French Bde.   – Front trench Z.3 – X.13.

   1st Div: Artillery   – Assist by similarly bombarding new front
      1 Battery   trench about G.4.

X Meerut Div: Art.
      1 Battery   – X.13 – M.10.

4. During the bombardment 3.30 – 4am the following tasks are allotted to the Howitzer batteries and section No 7 Mtn Batty.
   Canadian Div: Arty:
   ~~1 Battery 118th Bde~~   – ~~L.25~~
   ~~1 Battery 43rd Bde~~   – ~~K.13 – K.15.~~
   Siege Group.
   ~~37th Bde~~
   ~~1 Battery~~   – ~~K.13 – K.20~~
   ~~1 Battery~~   – ~~K.11 and K.21~~
   7th Siege Bde
      1st Battery   – VIOLAINES.
      56th Battery   – H.28
      81st Battery   – H.20
   No 7 Mtn Bty.
      1 Section   – CANTELEUX.

X 5. Ammunition allotted:–
   18 pdrs H.E. – 100 rounds per Battery
   Shrapnel as required.

X Meerut Battery – 90 rounds
                    ½ Shrapnel
                    ½ H.E.

continued

~~4.5" Hows - Shrapnel - 10 rounds per Battery.~~
6" Hows - Shrapnel - 8 rounds per Battery.
Section Mtn. Battery - 50 rounds.

[signature]
Major, R.A.
Brigade Major, Artillery, 4th Corps.

18-3-15.

SECRET.

TACTICAL PROGRESS REPORT
19th June 1915.

APPENDIX 269

1(a) ACTION BY OUR OWN ARTILLERY.

8.p.m. 18th June 1915. 8th Battery fired 3 rounds at party seen at newly wired trench 100 yards E. of FERME du BOIS.

3.30.a.m. to 3.40.a.m. 14th Battery bombarded trench X.16 to Z.3. with H.E. and shrapnel. At 3.43.a.m. to 3.53.a.m. searched 300 yards with shrapnel. At 3.53.a.m. to 4.a.m. resumed on trench with H.E. and shrapnel. Co-operation with IV Corps demonstration.

7.15.a.m. 66th Battery fired on sand-bagged house in retaliation for 77.mm. firing on our trenches. At three other times during the day same battery fired at same house in retaliation to Germans firing on our trenches.

12 noon. 14th Battery fired in retaliation on trenches S.W. of P.14.

3.30.a.m. Section of 55th Howitzer Battery registered P.14 and Q.15

5.15.p.m. 8th Battery fired shrapnel and H.E. at new wooden barricade half way between R.11 and R.13.

6.15.p.m. 7th Battery fired a few rounds to register the night night lines, having returned to MEERUT Division control from IV Corps.

6.55.p.m. 2nd Battery registered barricade in course of construction on LA QUINQUE RUE; obtaining 3 hits.

(b) ACTION BY HOSTILE ARTILLERY.

3.45.a.m. Guns at M.30 reported active, also some new flashes located 100 yards from M.30, N.E. along road.

3.45.a.m. 15.c.m. howitzer shelled vicinity L.8. in retaliation to the 3.30.a.m. bombardment of hostile trenches by IV Corps.

7.45.a.m. 77.mm. gun shelled vicinity X 23 d for about ½ hour. 15.c.m. howitzer shelled vicinity S 20 d for ½ hour, and M.5. for 15 minutes.

10.5.a.m. Heavy howitzer shelled PRINCES Road, probable direction LORGIES.

11.30.a.m. 10.c.m. howitzer shelled vicinity S 20 c 9'1 for over half an hour (BREWERY).

1.p.m. Some 77.mm. shell fired on trenches in front of SAVOY (S 9 c 5'0). Road in S 20 b shelled by howitzer-direction ILLIES.

2.30.p.m. 15.c.m. howitzer shelled vicinity DEAD COW FARM and communication trench near N.6.

2.37.p.m. Howitzer active on trenches of "A" Sub-section; supposed direction of LORGIES(?).

3.25.p.m. Howitzer shells were dropping in front of 14th Battery from direction of LORGIES(?).

3.30.p.m. 10.c.m. howitzer shelled vicinity X 6 a.

4.p.m. Two heavy howitzer shell fell short of 48th Heavy Battery.

2. INFORMATION.

AIRCRAFT:- 3.20.p.m. SAUSAGE Balloon seen at true bearing 119° from S 2 d 5'3. At 5.6.p.m. it ascended higher.

7.p.m. Two SAUSAGE Balloons seen true bearings 156° and 161° from M 32 c 10'8.

IDENTIFICATION:- 8.p.m. 18.6.15. 5 german soldiers and 2 Officers were seen in trench 100 yards E. of FERME du BOIS working. They had dark blue uniforms and dust cap covers with glazed peak.

DUMMIES:- Two dummies wearing service dress caps are placed close to parapet of Q.15 and on our side of it. These appear to be a dodge to find out whether men over parapet at Q.15 would draw fire from our trenches. Similar dummies were observed in front of another part of Q.15 on afternoon of 14th June.

Following extract from LAHORE Division Tactical Progress Report may prove of interest.

" Lieut ROSS 4th King's located through glasses what appeared to be a black sandbag with 2 small dots near the centre. A shot was fired at this sandbag which caused it to move. A second shot made it disappear. It is considered certain that this was a German look-out man with a black sandbag over his head and with 2 eyeholes cut in it for him to see through".

R H Lynch-Staunton Major R.A.

Brigade Major, Royal Artillery,
MEERUT DIVISION.

P.T.O

4th BRIGADE R.G.A. OPERATING ON OUR FRONT REPORT AS FOLLOWS:-

Engaged following during the day:-

A 6 a 7'7,　T 19 d 7'7,　T 10 a 0'5,　S 17 b 4'6,　S 17 b 4'6

The "Canon in Residence" is now believed to be in B 7 a.

"A" Form.   Army Form C. 2121.
MESSAGES AND SIGNALS.   No. of Message

Prefix	Code	m	Words	Charge	APPX 270 This message is on a/c of .... Service.	Recd. at 4.16 p.m.
Office of Origin and Service Instructions.			22			Date
			Sent At ... m. To ... By ...		(Signature of "Franking Officer.")	From By D Brown B.

TO   C R A Meerut

Sender's Number.	Day of Month.	In reply to Number	AAA
C 580	20th		

Indian Corps wires begins under instructions from 1st Army the 9th Bde RFA reverts to Indian Corps AAA Presume you do not desire brigade to move from present location ends AAA For report

War DIARY

From   Meerut Divn
Place
Time   4.45 pm

The above may be forwarded as now corrected.   (Z)

Censor.   Signature of Addressor or person authorised to telegraph in his name.
* This line should be erased if not required.

SECRET.

APPENDIX 271

TACTICAL PROGRESS REPORT
20th June 1915.

1(a) ACTION BY OUR OWN ARTILLERY.

7.35.p.m. 19th June 1915. 66th Battery fired at working party in trench S.W. of Q.12.

20th June 1915.

5.30.a.m. 14th Battery fired at M.12. and P.14. in retaliation for 77.mm. shelling our trenches.

9.55.a.m. 66th Battery fired at sand-bagged house S. of P.17 in reply to howitzer firing on our trenches.

12 noon. 8th Battery fired 5 rounds at barricade half way between R.11. and R.13.

14th Battery fired at M.20. - a gun firing from near this point.

2.30.p.m. and 3.15.p.m. 7th Battery fired a few rounds at houses near P.14 at request of Infantry, who reported snipers in that direction.

3.45.p.m. 14th Battery fired at P.14. to stop sniping.

4.45.p.m. 14th Battery registered house on right of M.23. 77.mm. thought to be firing from near there on St VAAST-RITZ Road- gun stopped at once.

5.30.p.m. 2nd Battery fired at hostile working party behind FERME du BOIS.

5.45.p.m. and 6.15.p.m. 8th Battery fired at German working party at Q.16.

(b) ACTION BY HOSTILE ARTILLERY.

9.30.a.m. Light howitzer shelled along the RUE du BOIS.

9.30.a.m. Heavy howitzer shelled the breastwork in rear of the "SAVOY"

10.a.m. 2 shell fell in vicinity of M 31 b.

11.a.m. to 11.20.a.m. 21.c.m. howitzer shelled vicinity of house 200 yards N. of M.7.

1.30.p.m. 10.5.c.m. howitzer shelled the BREWERY(S 20 c 10'3).

3.p.m. 10.5.c.m. howitzer shelled vicinity of REVOLVER HOUSE S 3 c 5.4.

3.30.p.m. 77.mm. shelled along the RUE du BOIS.

During the afternoon 10.5.c.m. howitzer and 77.mm. guns shelled the trenches intermittently, also 21.c.m. howitzer shelled FESTUBERT.

2. INFORMATION.

AIRCRAFT:- 6.a.m. Hostile aeroplane seen in vicinity of CROIX BARBEE, was turned back by our Anti Aircraft Guns.

Hostile SAUSAGE Balloons seen as under from M 32 a 4'7:-
8.45.a.m. true bearings 117½°. 9.20.a.m. two more 143½°. One of these came down 12.30.p.m.. 9.20.a.m. another observed 158½° went down 11.15.a.m. 10.a.m. another observed 144½° and another 157½°.

5.p.m. Hostile aeroplane up to left of 14th Battery. Was engaged by our Anti Aircraft Guns and retired in N.E. direction, returned several times towards RICHEBOURG.

5.45.p.m. German bi-plane engaged by Anti Aircraft guns and returned over BOIS du BIEZ.

5.55.p.m. German monoplane travelling S. over FERME du BOIS was engaged by our Anti Aircraft Guns.

6.20.p.m. German aeroplane up and was engaged by Anti Aircraft Guns.

6.40.p.m. Aeroplane East of CROIX BARBEE.

WIRE:- Fresh wire has been put up W. of white sand-bagged trench in FERME du BOIS.

R.K. Lynch-Staunton.
Major R.A.
Brigade Major, Royal Artillery,
MEERUT DIVISION.

1st BRIGADE R.G.A. OPERATING ON OUR FRONT REPORT:-

12.40.p.m. 8th Siege fired 3 rounds at T 10 c 2'0.

6.p.m. MOTHER took on an 8" howitzer at LA BASSEE (B 7 a 2'2)-one round reported within 10 yards and 3 within 25 yards.

6.35.p.m. 8" howitzer at WARNETON T 16 a 0'9 engaged by MOTHER. AIRMAN gave 2 hits on gun emplacement and one on Chateau-Range 9700.

P.T.O

4th BRIGADE R.G.A. OPERATING ON OUR FRONT REPORT:-

The following targets were engaged:-

T 10 a 0'6, T 15 d 0'4, T 19 d 7'7, S 24 b 0'10, T 20 a 5'1, T 19 a 0'1, T 20 b 2'1, T 19 d 9'9, S 24 b 2'2, S 18 b 5'3, T 19 a 2'2, S 17 b 4'6, S 12 central, LORGIES Cross Roads and gun at DISTILLERY.

"A" Form.   Army Form C. 2121.
MESSAGES AND SIGNALS.   No. of Message

Prefix Code m	Words	Charge	This message is on a/c of	Recd. at 8·9? m.
Office of Origin and Service Instructions.			APPENDIX 272 Service.	Date 21/6/15 From
	Sent At ___ m. To ___ By ___		(Signature of "Franking Officer.")	By G Gwynn Q

TO — CRA Meerut

Sender's Number.	Day of Month.	In reply to Number	AAA
* G617	21st		

Indian Corps G894 4·25 pm
begins Sixty first "How"
Battery leaves BALLEUL at
9pm 22nd inst to join
Indian Corps aaa Battery will
be attached to Meerut Div
on arrival aaa for
information and necessary
action.

From   Meerut Div
Place
Time   5·0 pm

The above may be forwarded as now corrected. (Z)

Censor. Signature of Addressor or person authorised to telegraph in his name.
* This line should be erased if not required.

"A" Form. Army Form C. 2121.
MESSAGES AND SIGNALS.

APPENDIX 273

Recd. at 5.12 P.m.
Date 21/6/15
From VII
By G. Grayson

TO — CRA Meerut

Sender's Number: G616
Day of Month: 21st
AAA

Indian Corps Wires G893 4.25 pm begins aaa Following moves will take place tomorrow aaa Section 55th How Bty from Meerut to 8th Divn aaa 10th WR How Bty from 8th Divn to 49th Divn aaa Both to move at eight pm aaa Details to be arranged between Divisions direct addressed Meerut 8th and 49th Divns ends for necessary action

Still on 5th copy
Go back to old place at POINT DE HEM

From Meerut Divn
Place
Time 5.0 pm

SECRET.   TACTICAL   PROGRESS   REPORT
                          21st June 1915.   APPENDIX 274

1(a) ACTION BY OUR OWN ARTILLERY.

7.35.p.m. 20th June 1915. 66th Battery fired at sand-bagged house S. of P.17 in retaliation to 77.mm. firing on our trenches- 77.mm. stopped firing.

21st June 1915:-

6.a.m. 8th Battery fired a few rounds at germans working at white sand-bag trench in Orchard of FERME du BOIS - repeated at 4.30.p.m. using a few H.E.

5.15.a.m. 66th Battery fired at sand-bagged house S. of P.17 in retaliation to 77.mm. firing on our trenches - 77.m.m. stopped firing.

12.30.p.m. 14th Battery fired at M.12 and M.14 in retaliation for 77.mm. shelling WINDY CORNER- 77.mm. stopped firing.

5.45.p.m. 7th Battery fired a few rounds near P.14 at request of Infantry- sniping reported from there.

8.25.p.m. 8th Battery fired 24 rounds at Q.15 Redoubt and communication trench, which were reported full of men by 1st Brigade R.G.A.

(b) ACTION BY HOSTILE ARTILLERY.

Enemy's Artillery very much more active to-day than it has been for many days.

During night 20th/21st Salvoes of 6 rounds were fired at odd intervals at communication trench in front of "SAVOY".

6.a.m. 77.mm. active on left of "D" Sub-section's trenches.

8.a.m. to 9.30.a.m. 15.c.m. howitzer shelled road M 27 d and road running N.W. - two houses were set on fire.

9.a.m. Heavy howitzers shelled vicinity of ROUGE CROIX.

Between 9.a.m. and 10.a.m. 10.5.c.m. howitzer shelled vicinity of PRINCE'S Road.

9.50.a.m. and 12 noon. German heavy howitzer(21.c.m.) shelled QUEEN MARY Road; real object appeared to be corner house S 2 c 3.3 on which a direct hit was obtained.

12 noon 10.5.c.m. howitzer shelled vicinity of WINDY CORNER.

12.30.p.m. About 12 heavy howitzer shell fell at road junction N. of SCHOOL HOUSE- RICHEBOURG.

12.45.p.m. Howitzers shelled tramway S.14.d 2.8 from direction of BOIS du BIEZ.

3.p.m. One 10.5.c.m. shell fell in 19th Battery position.

3.30.p.m. 77.mm. shelled vicinity S 13 b.

4.p.m. 10.5.c.m. howitzer and 77.mm. gun shelled trenches in front of INDIAN VILLAGE.

5.45.p.m. to 7.p.m. 15.c.m. howitzer shelled assembly trenches S. of CROIX BARBEE and vicinity of Anti Aircraft Section(probably with aeroplane observation).

6.p.m. 77.mm. shelled our trenches about V.2.

6.15.p.m. to 8.45.p.m. Germans firing salvoes and single rounds of 15.c.m. and 21.c.m. howitzers with aid of aeroplane at house M 32 b 2.2 and vicinity- about 40 rounds fired. Our Anti Aircraft gun did not open fire.

9.35.p.m. 77.mm. shelled communication trench in front of "SAVOY".

2. INFORMATION.

AIRCRAFT:- 4.20.a.m. Hostile aeroplane over CROIX BARBEE flying North.

7.50.a.m. Hostile aeroplane reconnoitring over CROIX BARBEE.

8.15.a.m. Hostile aeroplane flying N.E. to S.E. of CROIX BARBEE- engaged by Anti Aircraft.

8.40.a.m. Hostile aeroplane dropped 3 white lights in vicinity of german lines.

9.45.a.m. SAUSAGE Balloon up true bearing 120° from M 26 c 5.1.

9.50.a.m. Hostile aeroplane over CHOCOLAT MENIER CORNER flying South. Was engaged by our Anti Aircraft guns.

5.50.p.m. German aeroplane over PORT ARTHUR dropping lights, observing for heavy howitzer shelling CROIX BARBEE. Anti Aircraft Section was driven out of its position. A blind shell "scoop" gave true bearing of 110° from M 32 b 3.4.

6.15.p.m. Hostile aeroplane observing over WINDY CORNER. A second one appeared on left flank at 6.30.p.m.

P.T.O.

OBSERVATION POST:- FORFAR Battery reports seeing people continually going into sand-bagged house about P.18(S. of P.17 ?) and concludes it is being used as an O.P.

SPECIAL:- LA BASSEE Church Tower has been completely knocked down - the church itself still standing. Tower of TOWN HALL is also reported to have disappeared.

R. K. Lynch-Staunton.
Major R.A.

Brigade Major, Royal Artillery,
MEERUT DIVISION.

1st BRIGADE R.G.A. OPERATING ON OUR FRONT REPORT:-

8th Siege Battery shelled ILLIES and LORGIES.

4th BRIGADE R.G.A. OPERATING ON OUR FRONT REPORT:-

48th Heavy Battery:-

Engaged S 30 b 2'2, T 20 a 0'6, T 10 a 0'6, A 6 a 7'7,

T 25 c 7'7, A 6 d 4'1, S 30 central, ILLIES CHURCH, T 19 d 7'7

8.50.p.m. Engaged T 10 a 0'6 now identified as the battery of 3 guns which had been crumping all day with a wireless aeroplane.

109th Heavy Battery:-

Fired at Chateau WARNETON and S 17 b 4'2.

110th Heavy Battery:-

Fired at CHATEAU WARNETON, S 23 c 9'1, T 19 a 2'2, T 20 a 5'1.

APPENDIX 274a

4th CORPS ARTILLERY

Instructions No. 9.

DEFENCE.

1. The Canadian Division now hold the front line from the Canal to a point where "Grenadier Road" meets the British Trenches about 100 yards North of I.5.
The 7th Division continues the line to a point about 250 yards North of L.8, where the ditch J.11 - Z.1 cuts our front line.
The 51st Division continues the line to LA QUINQUE RUE.

2. The ARTILLERY of the CANADIAN DIVISION will from 8 p.m. to-night be responsible for the security of the front of its own Division and will have as its zone the enemy Trenches and defences between the Canal and J.11.

3. The ALEXANDER GROUP will be responsible for the security of the right half of the 7th Division. Zone J.11 - K.6.

4. The NICHOLSON GROUP will be responsible for the security of the left half of the 7th Division and for the right of the 51st Division. Zone K.6 - Z.3 - X.16.
This Group will furnish a F.O.O. to the headquarters of the Right Battalion of the 51st Division by night, and will ensure the necessary inter-communication by day.
The group will also furnish an Officer to the Battalion holding the left half of the 7th Division front.

5. The remainder of the front of the 51st DIVISION will be covered thus:-
   (a) X.16 - M.10   French Brigade, 51st Div.
   (b) From 100 yards W.   The MEERUT Divisional Artillery
       of M.10 - M.10 -   (Indian Corps) assumes responsibility
       Northwards.   for Artillery support of the British
                                    line.
   (c) 1st Highland Bde.   Zone X.21 - X.25.
   (d) 2nd Highland Bde.   Zone X.18 - 19 . 20.

6. Each Artillery unit will be prepared to bring fire to bear at once, if required, on the flanks of and approaches to the zone on either side of it.

                                              Major, R.A.

21-6-15.   Brigade Major, Artillery, 4th Corps.

B.G.C.R.A.
   Meerut Div
      Forwarded. Does this meet with your approval, please.

                                       Noel Birch
                                       Brig. Genl.
21.6.15.   C.R.A. 4th Corps.

APPENDIX 274(b)

No.765-R.A.(L).   Headquarters Divisional Artillery,
                                     MEERUT DIVISION.

CONFIDENTIAL.   21st June 1915.

To,

   The Commanding Royal Artillery,

        7th Division.

   Reference your instructions No.9 dated 21st June 1915, paragraph 5(b), I wish to point out the 9th Brigade R.F.A. is for to-night acting under the orders of C.R.A., HIGHLAND Division, and I am informed he has allotted them to cover the frontage L.10 to M.10.

   From noon tomorrow 22nd June 1915, the 28th Battery (9th Brigade) only will remain at the disposal of C.R.A. HIGHLAND Division. No responsibility for covering the frontage named can be accepted by the MEERUT Divisional Artillery, who are only responsible for their own front as far Southwards as QUINQUE RUE.

                                R. St. Lecky Brigadier General R.A.
                         Commanding Royal Artillery, MEERUT Division.

APPENDIX 275

SECRET.

TACTICAL PROGRESS REPORT
22nd June 1915.

1(a). ACTION BY OUR OWN ARTILLERY.

7.30.p.m. 21st June 1915. 14th Battery fired at working party in trench S.W. of P.14; party dispersed at a double.
8.p.m. 21st June 1915. 14th Battery fired at trench (working party) 50 yards W. of P.14.
8.30.p.m. 21st June 1915. 8th Battery fired 24 rounds at Q.15 to Q.11; germans reported collecting in trench.
22nd June 1915:-
9.a.m. 2nd Battery fired 6 rounds at a party of germans behind FERME du BOIS.
10.15.a.m. 14th Battery shelled M.23 and behind M.26 in retaliation to 77.mm. firing on S 7 b- which stopped it firing.
11.a.m. 44th Battery registered trench E. of COUR d'AVOUE.
5.p.m. 8th Battery fired a few rounds at germans seen in white sand bag trench FERME du BOIS.
8.50.p.m. 2nd Battery fired 2 salvoes at Q.15 where enemy were reported in large numbers.

(b) ACTION BY HOSTILE ARTILLERY.

7.30.a.m. 15.c.m. howitzer shelled vicinity X 18 a and S 13 b heavily for over an hour; a burst of 3 and 4 to start with and finishing up with two bursts of 10 rounds each, firing altogether about 100 rounds. Shell scoop from X 18 a 5'5 gave true bearing of 99°.
7.45.a.m. Heavy gun fired on road about S 14 d 7'3 from direction of BOIS du BIEZ.
8.15.a.m. to 8.45.a.m. About 20(15.c.m.) shell fell in vicinity of M 32 c 2'3.
8.25.a.m. Heavy howitzers shelled tram line and first aid post in PRINCES ROAD, also communication trench on right of "A" Sub-section and support trench of left of "A" Sub-section. At least 3 hostile batteries were firing. Aeroplane audible but not visible.
9.15.a.m. 15.c.m. howitzer shelled RICHEBOURG and vicinity-observation by aeroplane over RICHEBOURG.
9.30.a.m. Heavy howitzer shelled South corner of RICHEBOURG.
10.15.a.m. 77.mm. shelled 19th Battery position, obtaining a good bracket- no damage.
6.20.p.m. Shell(?) dropped in field 200 yards W. of 28th Battery position, slightly wounding a French woman working in the field; thought to be a bomb, but may have been german Archie shell- no aeroplane visible, or any shelling seen at this time.
7.10.p.m. Hostile howitzer shelled trenches of 3rd LONDON's, in reply to shelling of Q.15 by 8th Siege Battery, they dropped one shell into FERME du BOIS.

2. INFORMATION.

AIRCRAFT:- 6.30.a.m. Hostile aeroplane seen very high up over RUE des CHEVATTES.
7.24.a.m. Hostile aeroplane circling in front of 66th Battery apparently observing for heavy howitzer.
8.12.a.m. Hostile aeroplane circling in front of 14th Battery.
8.40.a.m. Hostile aeroplane near 44th Battery ranging for german Artillery.
9.15.a.m. Hostile bi-plane flew N.W. over LA COUTURE, was engaged and turned East.
9.30.a.m. Hostile SAUSAGE Balloon up true bearing $119\frac{1}{2}°$ from M 32 a 2'8- descended at 10.15.a.m.
10.20.a.m. Hostile SAUSAGE Balloon up true bearing 135° from M 32 a 2'8- remained up 30 minutes.
6.15.p.m. Hostile aeroplane reconnoitring over 14th Battery O.P.
MOVEMENTS:- 4.a.m. 3 germans seen to leave FERME COUR d'AVOUNE in direction of Q.16.
Germans seen walking in white sandbag trench 150 yards N. of Q.16, and in trench in rear near Q.16.
8.p.m. 5 germans seen in marching order going back along communicating trench from P.18-possibly relief.

P.T.O.

WIRE:- Fresh wire W. of white sand bag trench 150 yards N. of Q.16.
BOMB GUN:- A new bomb gun is thought to be somewhere South of COUR d'AVOINE.
RELIEFS:- During the afternoon the 9th Brigade R.F.A. relieved the 4th Brigade R.F.A. of the Artillery support of the DEHRA DUN Brigade.

Near Q.15 there is a small weather cock.

R. K. Lynch-Staunton.
Major R.A.

Brigade Major, Royal Artillery,
MEERUT DIVISION.

SECRET

APPENDIX 276

OPERATION ORDER NO 39.   Copy No......

Sir   by
Lieutenant-General/C.A. ANDERSON, K.C.B.,
                Commanding Meerut Division.

Reference:-   23rd June 1915.
    Special Trench Map.

1. The following re-adjustment of the line will be carried out
    tonight.
    (a) DEHRA DUN Brigade will, in addition to its present front,
        take over from GARHWAL Brigade the line up to, and including,
        R.5, and FARM CORNER. The communication trench from R.5.
        back to the old British line will remain to GARHWAL Brigade.

    (b) GARHWAL Brigade will hand over the portion of the line as
        above to DEHRA DUN Brigade and will take over the line from
        JULLUNDER and FEROZEPORE Brigades up to and including the
        ORCHARD in S.10.A.b, and PEAR STREET Communication trench.

2. Arrangements for these reliefs will be made by Brigadiers
    concerned and reported to Divisional Headquarters.
        The hours at which reliefs are completed and command of the
    new line assumed will be similarly reported.

3. G.O.C. Meerut Division will assume command of the new front at
    6-0.a.m. on 24th June.

                                                    A.T.Aris
                                                    Major.
                                                General Staff.
Issued to Signal Company for despatch   MEERUT Division.
at 4-0.p.m.

Copy No 1 to Indian Corps.
    ,, ,, 2   Dehra Dun Brigade.
           3   Garhwal Brigade.
           4   Bareilly Brigade.
           5   C.R.A. Meerut.
           6   C.R.E. Meerut.
           7   4th Indian Cavalry.
           8   107th Pioneers.
           9   Meerut Signal Company.
          10   Lahore Division.
          11   51st (Highland) Division.
          12   A.A. & Q.M.G.

Secret
BM 892

APPENDIX 27/90
Meerut Div Arty

To
GOC RA, Lahore Div

Meerut Div is relieving our
frontage V.1 to ORCHARD
S 10 f from LAHORE DIV
tonight.

Would you kindly arrange for the
Artillery support on their front
until I can get 9th Battery
to do this.

If so, will you please mobilise
said Battery to establish
LIASON with the Infantry
Battalion remainder of the
GARHWAL Bde which take
over this portion from the
LAHORE DIV tonight?

By Motor Cyclist.
5-20 pm
23/6/15

R M Syed-French
Major RA
for C.R.A. Meerut Div

Secret

APPENDIX 278
B.M. 102
23-6-915

Meerut Divn in Artillery Arrangements have been made to cover front VI to East end of ORCHARD (S.10.b) with the whole of the 18th Brigade (3 Battns). This arrangement will stand until something else is arranged with you.

McWalter Capt
M. Rock?
Lahn

APPENDIX 279

SECRET.

TACTICAL PROGRESS REPORT
23rd June 1915.

1(a) ACTION BY OUR OWN ARTILLERY.

A very quiet day.

8th Battery fired 5 rounds at germans seen working between V.2 and R.8.
6.30.p.m. 20th Battery fired on house at X 29 which appeared occupied.

(b) ACTION BY HOSTILE ARTILLERY.

7.30.a.m. 77.mm. gun shelled CHOCOLAT MENIER CORNER from direction of RUE du MARAIS cross roads.
4.p.m. 10.5.c.m. howitzer shelled PRINCES ROAD and OLD BRITISH Trench S 15 for half an hour.
6.15.p.m. 10.5.c.m. howitzer fired on our Reserve trenches from P.3. to about 100 yards W. of L.4.
7.p.m. 15.c.m. howitzer shelled vicinity of LA COUTURE.

2. INFORMATION.

OBSERVATION POST:- House at M.12 appears a very likely O.P. and would be much improved by a few heavy H.E. shell.
EARTHWORK:- There appears to be a very elaborate earthwork about X.30.
AIRCRAFT:- None reported.

R.K. Lynch-Staunton
Major R.A.
Brigade Major, Royal Artillery
MEERUT DIVISION.

1st BRIGADE R.G.A. OPERATING ON OUR FRONT REPORT:-

8th Siege Battery took on T 25 b 8'5 in reply to morning "crumping".

4th BRIGADE R.G.A. OPERATING ON OUR FRONT REPORT:-

Some "crumping" in the morning, but very difficult to locate owing to mist; some 77.mm. also active.
12.35.p.m. 110th Heavy Battery engaged T 14 c 10'0 thought to be active.
12.45.p.m. WARNETON battery active towards QUINQUE RUE- 48th and 110th Heavy Batteries fired at him and he shut down.
2.40.p.m. 110th Heavy Battery engaged S 23 c 9'2 active 77.mm.
4.18.p.m. 48th Heavy Battery fired at T 10 a 0'6 (15.c.m. howitzer) and stopped him.
4.50.p.m. 110th Heavy Battery re-engaged WARNETON and 48th Heavy Battery took on S 23 c 9'1 active on RITZ and soon stopped him.
4.55.p.m. Engaged S 24 central.
5.15.p.m. "Canon in Residence" active and engaged by a lot of batteries but in spite of it service continued; his is apparently a stout pulpit and an aeroplane is needed to unfrock him.
4.45.p.m. 48th Heavy Battery took on Q.15 and got several in Redoubt and trench. 10th Siege Observing Officer directing with success.

SECRET.

APPENDIX 280

TACTICAL PROGRESS REPORT
24th June 1915.

1(a) ACTION BY OUR OWN ARTILLERY:-
10.10.a.m. 2nd Battery fired a few rounds to make some adjustments in present night lines.
12 noon. 44th Battery registered on new night lines.
12.30.p.m. 20th Battery fired a few rounds on enemy's trench opposite P.11 in retaliation for their shelling our front and support trenches at P.10.
4.p.m. 2nd Battery fired a few rounds at DISTILLERY to check enemy shelling our trenches.
4.30.p.m. 8th Battery registered on new night lines Q.16-Q.11.
5.5.p.m. 2nd Battery checked registrations in order to be able to take up new night lines when required.

(b) ACTION BY HOSTILE ARTILLERY.
Heavy howitzer shell fired at various points throughout the day.
12.30.p.m. 77.mm. fired on our trenches and at other hours of the afternoon.
1.p.m. 21.c.m.(?) howitzer shelled our support trenches in front of TROCADERO (X 18 c 5'8).
Between 2.p.m. and 3.p.m. 15.c.m. howitzer shelled new fire trench W. of FARM CORNER; apparently registering it.

2. INFORMATION:-
MOVEMENTS:- Several germans seen working, one in white shirt, in their Reserve trench near R.9.

R.K. Lynch-Staunton.
Major R.A.
Brigade Major, Royal Artillery,
MEERUT DIVISION.

1st BRIGADE R.G.A. OPERATING ON OUR FRONT REPORT:-

5.30.p.m. 2 guns of 8th Siege joined in with 48th, 109th and 110th Heavy Batteries in a salvo on T 19 d 7'7 which had been offensive during the day.
7.p.m. One round fired at FOURNES in reply to shelling of LA COUTURE; repeated at 7.40.p.m. and again at 8.p.m.

4th BRIGADE R.G.A. OPERATING ON OUR FRONT REPORT:-

A quiet and misty morning 110th Heavy Battery engaged S 24 central, S 23 c 9'2.
1.p.m. Following targets engaged T 4 d 3'5, T 10 a 0'6, S 12 b 5'0 and S 6 d 7'4 – on the last with the 6th round (48th H.B.) sent up a huge column of smoke, which was not the shell burst- this proves these pits are now occupied. H.B.C.
2.45.p.m. LORGIES howitzer active-110th H.B. tried T 19 a 2'8 successfully.
2.50.p.m. Two howitzers active on the RUE du BOIS from T 20 a 8'2-stopped by 48th H.B.; 110th H.B. engaged T 4 d 3'5.
3.15.p.m. Crumps falling near DEHRA DUN Headquarters, 110th H.B. tried WARNETON and 48th T 19 d 7'7. H.B.C.
3.45.p.m. and 5.20.p.m. 109th and 110th H.B's engaged the DISTILLERY S 17 central at request of 2nd Battery R.F.A.
5.10.p.m. 110th H.B. engaged S 17 b 1'9   77.m.m. probably a new position.
5.30.p.m. 48th, 109th and 110th H.B's had a salvo at T 19 d 7'7 a very troublesome howitzer battery.

APPENDIX 281

SECRET.

TACTICAL PROGRESS REPORT
25th June 1915.

1(a) ACTION BY OUR OWN ARTILLERY.

3.30.p.m. 44th Battery registered trenches near P.14 for now line.
5.15.p.m. 8th Battery registered trench W. of FERME COUR d'AVOUE (new front).
6.p.m. 2nd Battery checked registration on new front.
61st Howitzer Battery carried out registration during the day.

(b) ACTION BY HOSTILE ARTILLERY.

7.45.p.m. 24th June 1915. An odd shell, now and then, from a 10.5.c.m. howitzer fell in vicinity of Tram Terminus in KING'S ROAD.
25th June 1915:-
5.p.m. 15.c.m. howitzer shelled FESTUBERT and 10.5.c.m. howitzer shelled our trenches in vicinity of M.9.
5.35.p.m. 15.c.m. howitzer shelled RUE du BOIS at junction of road at S 15 a.
6.p.m. Heavy howitzer shelled PRINCES ROAD and CHOCOLAT MENIER CORNER.
6.30.p.m. 77.mm. shelled between RICHEBOURG and LA COUTURE - mostly blind shell.
6.45.p.m. 10.5.c.m. howitzer shelled vicinity X 17 b.

2. INFORMATION.

RELIEFS:- Pending relief of HIGHLAND Division on our right 9th Brigade R.F.A. which had established Liason with DEHRA DUN Brigade took over support of HIGHLAND Division (frontage X.16 to QUINQUE RUE. Similarly 13th Brigade R.F.A. which had been supporting GARHWAL Brigade established Liason with DEHRA DUN Brigade (QUINQUE RUE to R.5.), while 18th Brigade R.F.A. of LAHORE Division assumed responsibility for support of GARHWAL Brigade (R.5 to ORCHARD(S 10 b) inclusive).
All the above as a temporary measure only.
61st Howitzer Battery joined MEERUT Division from YPRES and went into action in same Orchard as 19th Battery R.F.A.

AIRCRAFT:- 7.15.p.m. 24th June 1915 Aeroplane of doubtful nationality flew N. over LA COUTURE.
25th June 1915:- None reported.

R. K. Lynch-Staunton.
Major R.A.

Brigade Major, Royal Artillery,
MEERUT DIVISION.

APPENDIX 281(a)

OPERATION ORDER NO 40 Copy No...7......
by
LIEUTENANT GENERAL SIR C.A. ANDERSON, K.C.B.,
Commanding MEERUT Division.

Reference:-
Trench map 1:10000.   25th June 1915.

RELIEF.   1. The BAREILLY BRIGADE will relieve the GARHWAL BRIGADE
               in the trenches on the night 28th/29th June. All details
               to be arranged between Brigadiers concerned.

BILLETS.   2. Brigade Headquarters will be exchanged and the GARHWAL
               BRIGADE will move into the billets now occupied by the
               BAREILLY BRIGADE as Divisional Reserve. State of readiness -
               2 hours' notice.

TRENCH   3. GARHWAL BRIGADE will hand over the trench mortars in
STORES.   line and the Hyposcope Rifle on charge as well as any
               trench stores surplus to their allotment to BAREILLY
               BRIGADE.

REPORTS.   4. Reports to CHATEAU DE LA RAULT.

                                                    Norie.
                                                    Colonel.
                                                    General Staff.
                                                    MEERUT Division.

Issued to Signal Company for despatch
at 1-0.p.m.

Copy No 1 and 2 to Indian Corps.
 ,,   ,,   3   ,, Lahore Division.
 ,,   ,,   4   ,, Dehra Dun Brigade.
 ,,   ,,   5   ,, Garhwal Brigade.
 ,,   ,,   6   ,, Bareilly Brigade.
 ,,   ,,   7   ,, C.R.A. Meerut.
 ,,   ,,   8   ,, C.R.E. Meerut.
 ,,   ,,   9   ,, 4th Indian Cavalry.
 ,,   ,,   10   ,, 107th Pioneers.
 ,,   ,,   11   ,, Meerut Train.
 ,,   ,,   12   ,, Meerut Signals.
 ,,   ,,   13   ,, A.D.M.S. Meerut.
 ,,   ,,   14   ,, A.A. &. Q.M.G.
 ,,   ,,   15   ,, D.A.A.& Q.M.G.
 ,,   ,,   16   ,, D.A.A.G.
 ,,   ,,   17 to 23 War Diary and Files.

APPENDIX 281(?)

No. 770-R.A.(L). Headquarters Divisional Artillery,
MEERUT Division.

25th June 1915.

SECRET.

To,

The Officers Commanding,
4th Brigade R.F.A.
9th Brigade R.F.A.
13th Brigade R.F.A.
61st Howitzer Battery R.F.A.

The following extract from MEERUT DIVISION Operation Order No.40 dated the 25th June 1915, is forwarded for information and such action as necessary:-

x x x   x x x

RELIEF. 1. The BAREILLY Brigade will relieve the GARHWAL Brigade in the trenches on the night 28th/29th June. All details to be arranged between Brigadiers concerned.

BILLETS. 2. Brigade Headquarters will be exchanged and the GARHWAL Brigade will move into the billets now occupied by the BAREILLY Brigade as Divisional Reserve. State of readiness 2 hour's notice.

x x x   x x x

Major R.A.
Brigade Major, Royal Artillery,
MEERUT DIVISION.

SECRET.

APPENDIX 282

TACTICAL PROGRESS REPORT
26th June 1915

1(a) <u>ACTION BY OUR OWN ARTILLERY.</u>

11.30.a.m. 44th Battery registered X.31, X.32 to P.14- new frontage.
5.45.p.m. 2nd Battery fired 50 H.E. on two points near Q.15. These points were indicated by O.C. 2nd 2nd Gurkhas. The trench in the vicinity of these points was repeatedly hit and planks etc., thrown up.
During the afternoon the 28th Battery registered N.15 and M.14- 4 direct hits on M.14(an O.P.).

(b) <u>ACTION BY HOSTILE ARTILLERY.</u>

21.c.m. howitzer shelled FESTUBERT continually during the day.
8.30.a.m. 15.c.m. howitzer shelled vicinity of RUE du BOIS-RUE de l'EPINETTE Cross Roads(a few rounds).
8.40.a.m. 77.mm. gun shelled our trenches in vicinity of M.9. from direction of VIOLAINES.
11.a.m. 77.mm. shelled trenches on front of INDIAN VILLAGE for about 20 minutes.
11.30.a.m. 21.c.m. howitzer shelled FESTUBERT-5 rounds out of 10 were blind.
11.45.a.m. 77.mm. shelled trenches in front of SAVOY.
12.15.p.m. 15.c.m. howitzer shelled vicinity X 18 c(a few rounds)
1.45.p.m. 10.5.c.m. howitzer shelled vicinity X 17 d for about 20 minutes-(a few rounds).
2.p.m. 10.5.c.m. howitzer shelled REVOLVER HOUSE.
2.30.p.m. 77.mm. shelled RUE du BOIS.
4.20.p.m. 77.mm. shelled vicinity X 18 c(a few rounds).
6.p.m. Heavy howitzer and 77.mm. shelled our trenches in retaliation for 2nd Battery firing on Q.15 with H.E..
Front trench M.9. and M.8. shelled intermittently by 10.5.c.m. howitzer during the afternoon.

2. <u>INFORMATION.</u>

<u>AIRCRAFT</u>:- Three German SAUSAGE Balloons were up during the day.
9.15.a.m. Hostile aeroplane flying W. over CHOCOLAT MENIER CORNER- was engaged by "Archie" and turned E. Same aeroplane returned 10 minutes later with same result.
9.30.a.m. "Wireless" german aeroplane up.
9.45.a.m. Hostile aeroplane seen flying North.
The French Observation balloon East of BETHUNE was shelled at 11a.m.- fire appeared effective and balloon descended at 11.30.a.m.
8.35.p.m. ZEPPELIN reported over LORETTE Spur travelling East.

R.K. Lynch-Staunton.

Major R.A.
Brigade Major, Royal Artillery,
MEERUT DIVISION.

4th BRIGADE R.G.A. OPERATING ON OUR FRONT REPORT:-

9.30.a.m. 110th H.B. engaged 77.mm. at S 17 b 1'8.
10.15.a.m. 48th H.B. engaged A 6 a 7'7 reported active. This position is now believed to be occupied by 77.m.m. "The Canon" having moved to B 7 a. Same again at 12.20.p.m. with success.
2.15.p.m. 110th H.E. put down S 11 d 2'2.
3.5.p.m. 110th H.B. fired at S 12 central on 77.mm. active thereabouts- effect good and battery shut down.
3.20.p.m. 48th H.B. engaged LORGIES Church suspected of sheltering enemys observer and again at 5.15.p.m.
4.5.p.m. Engaged S 30 central and S 29 b 2'3 active.
6.3.p.m. Engaged S 3 c 8'7 and S 15 a 6'6.
8.30.p.m. 109th H.B. engaged T 1 d central shelling towards LAVENTIE.

SECRET.   APPENDIX 283

TACTICAL PROGRESS REPORT
27th June 1915.

1(a) ACTION BY OUR OWN ARTILLERY.

10.45.a.m. 2nd Battery fired a few rounds at FERME COUR d'
AVOUE, where movement was seen.
1.30.p.m. 44th Battery fired at trench on LA QUINQUE RUE,
on suspicion of a bomb gun which had annoyed the 1st 9th
Gurkhas.
5.p.m. 2nd Battery engaged trenches near Q.15 in retaliation
for enemy shelling our fire and support trenches.

(b) ACTION BY HOSTILE ARTILLERY.

8.30.a.m. 10.5.c.m. howitzer shelled trenches in vicinity of
P.7 and P.6.
15.c.m. howitzer shelled RUE du BOIS - RUE de l'EPINETTE
Cross Roads (a few rounds).
9.40.a.m. 10.5.c.m. howitzer shelled CHOCOLAT MENIER CORNER
(about 20 rounds) from direction of LORGIES.
12 noon. Heavy howitzer shelled corner of ALBERT ROAD and
RUE du BOIS.
12.30.p.m. 15.c.m. howitzer began shelling Cross Roads S 15 a
and then switched to CHOCOLAT MENIER CORNER.
O.P. of 20th Battery was knocked down- about 60 rounds were
fired from direction of VIOLAINES- no casualties.
4.40.p.m. 15.c.m. howitzer shelled trenches in vicinity of M.9.
5.p.m. Three 77.mm. shell fell 150 yards in front of 44th
Battery.   77.mm. shelled fire and support trenches in
front of SAVOY.
6.30.p.m. About 9 heavy howitzer)(probably 21.c.m.)fired at
RICHEBOURG Church.

2. INFORMATION.
AIRCRAFT;- Hostile Sausage balloon up at 9.10.a.m. true bearing 114° 40' from M 32 a 3'7.
BOMBARDMENT of 26.6.15:- O.C. 2nd 2nd Gurkhas reports that
2nd Battery bombardment of yesterday(50 H.E.) was very effective and that the bomb guns have moved from his area.   He
states that such retaliation has an excellent moral effect
on his own men and thinks that a similar procedure should be
adopted if his trenches are really heavily shelled.

                                          Major R.A.
                        Brigade Major, Royal Artillery,
                              MEERUT DIVISION.

1st BRIGADE R.G.A. OPERATING ON OUR FRONT REPORT:-

12.30.p.m. 8th Siege in reply to shelling of S 8 d and S 15 engaged
A 12 d 3'7 which was active. H.B.C. after 5 rounds had been fired.
5.45.p.m. Replied to "crumping" of LA COUTURE by shelling FOURNES.

4th BRIGADE R.G.A. OPERATING ON OUR FRONT REPORT:-

8.45.a.m. 48th took on T 10 a 0'6 in reply to heavy how: on S 10.
9.45.a.m. 48th took on A 6 a 7'7 shelling S 15.
1.58.p.m. 48th fired on ILLIES(at a counter irritant).
2.5.p.m. 48th engaged trench K.7 - X.5 with H.E. at order of No.1
Group- observation not possible as lines broken, but a pious hope
that much damage was done as it had been well registered.
4.40.p.m. 110th engaged A 6 a 7'7 and again at 6.17.p.m.
5.30.p.m. In reply to evening "hate" on LA COUTURE 48th tried
HALPEGARDE.
6.30.p.m. 109th tried T 19 d 7'7 a possible culprit and 48th had
a go at ILLIES.
HUN Shelling:- 8.a.m. Howitzer from ILLIES on fields behind "RITZ"-
4 blinds.
12 noon. How: from VIOLAINES on an O.P. 150 yds S.W. of SAVOY-30
rounds of 15.c.m. and 10 blinds.
2.30.p.m. How: N. of ILLIES on RUE de l'EPINETTE.
Several 77.mm. during day from VIOLAINES.
A 3 a 7'7 has a howitzer thereabouts still.

APPENDIX 283(a)

(MEERUT DIVISION OPERATION ORDER No. 40 IS SUPERSEDED)

OPERATION OORDER No. 41   Copy No. 6

by

Lieutenant-General Sir Charles ANDERSON, K.C.B.,
Commanding MEERUT DIVISION.

Reference map:-
FRANCE - BETHUNE - 1:40,000 &
Special Trench Map.

27th June 1915.

Extension of Frontage & Area.
1. The Meerut Division front is extended to the North to the ESTAIRES - LA BASSEE Road exclusive.
The boundaries of the billeting area are modified:-
On the north to the line LA BASSEE Road - RUE DU BOIS junction exclusive - Road junction S.4.a.8.9. exclusive - our present line at ST VAAST.
ON the South to L'EPINETTE - RUE DU BOIS Road junction inclusive - thence through X.17.a.10.3 - X.10.b.2.5 and R.32.c.7.0, where the old boundary is resumed.

Reliefs.
2. Bareilly Brigade on the night 28th/29th June will take over from Garhwal Brigade the front from BOND STREET Communication Trench exclusive to the Orchard Post inclusive, and from Ferozepore Brigade from ORCHARD Post exclusive to the ESTAIRES - LA BASSEE Road exclusive.
All details to be arranged between Brigadiers concerned.
The LOCON-LESTREM Road is not available for the use of Meerut Divn troops between 9.30 and 11.0 P.M.
The G.O.C. Bareilly Bde will take over command of his new front as soon as the relief is completed.

Bde Hdqrs.
3. G.O.C. Garhwal Bde will retain his present Hdqrs; Bde HQ in farm at M.32.d.7.8 Hdqrs for Bareilly Bde will be established X.17.a.10.3.

Trench Stores.
4. The trench mortars will be emplaced by the Divisional Bomb-gun Officer in consultation with Brigadiers.

Divisional Reserve.
5. The G.O.C. Garhwal Bde will detail one British and two Indian Battalions as Divisional Reserve, to be billetted in LES LOBES, R.28.d. and R.34.b. State of readiness - two hours notice.

Reports.
6. Reports to CHATEAU DE LA RAULT.

Colonel,
General Staff.

Headquarters, Meerut Division.
28th June 1915.

G.800

Reference:-
Meerut Division Operation Order No. 41.

No. G.766 is cancelled. Para 3 should now read as follows:-

"G.Os C. Garhwal and Dehra Dun Brigades will retain their present headquarters. Bareilly Brigade Headquarters will be in farm at M.32.d.7/8."

Addressed all concerned.

Colonel,
General Staff.

APPENDIX 283(a)

(MEERUT DIVISION OPERATION ORDER No. 40 IS SUPERSEDED)

OPERATION ORDER No. 41   Copy No. 6
by
Lieutenant-General Sir Charles ANDERSON, K.C.B.,
Commanding MEERUT DIVISION.

Reference map:-
FRANCE - BETHUNE - 1:40000 &
Special Trench Map.

27th June 1915.

Extension of Frontage & Area.

1. The Meerut Division front is extended to the North to the ESTAIRES - LA BASSEE Road exclusive.
   The boundaries of the billeting area are modified:-
   On the north to the line LA BASSEE Road - RUE DU BOIS junction exclusive - Road junction S.4.a.8.9. exclusive - our present line at ST VAAST.
   ON the South to L'EPINETTE - RUE DU BOIS Road junction inclusive - thence through X.17.a.10.3 - X.10.b.2.5 and R.32.c.7.0, where the old boundary is resumed.

Reliefs.

2. Bareilly Brigade on the night 28th/29th June will take over from Garhwal Brigade the front from BOND STREET Communication Trench exclusive to the Orchard Post inclusive, and from Ferozepore Brigade from ORCHARD Post exclusive to the ESTAIRES - LA BASSEE Road exclusive.
   All details to be arranged between Brigadiers concerned.
   The LOCON-LESTREM Road is not available for the use of Meerut Divn troops between 9.30 and 11.0 P.M.
   The G.O.C. Bareilly Bde will take over command of his new front as soon as the relief is completed.

Bde Hdqrs.

3. G.O.C. Garhwal Bde will retain his present Hdqrs; Bde HQ in farm Hdqrs for Bareilly Bde will be established at X.17.a.10.3. at M.32.d.7.8

Trench Stores.

4. The trench mortars will be emplaced by the Divisional Bomb-gun Officer in consultation with Brigadiers.

Divisional Reserve.

5. The G.O.C. Garhwal Bde will detail one British and two Indian Battalions as Divisional Reserve, to be billetted in LES LOBES, R.28.d. and R.34.b. State of readiness - two hours notice.

Reports.

6. Reports to CHATEAU DE LA RAULT.

C.Norie
Colonel,
General Staff,
MEERUT DIVISION.

Issued at 3.15 P.M. to Signals for distribution:-

Copy No. 1 to Indian Corps
2   Lahore Divn
3   Dehra Dun Bde
4   Garhwal Bde
5   Bareilly Bde
6   C.R.A. Meerut
7   C.R.E. Meerut
8   4th Ind. Cavalry
9   107th Pioneers
10 Meerut Train
11 Meerut Signals
12 to A.D.M.S. Meerut
13   A.A.& Q.M.G.
14   D.A.A.& Q.M.G.
15   D.A.A.G.
16 to Diary & files
24

APPENDIX 283(F)

No.777-R.A.(L).　　　　　　　Headquarters Divisional Artillery,
　　　　　　　　　　　　　　　　MEERUT DIVISION.

　　　　　　　　　　　　　　　　28th June 1915.

SECRET.

　　　To,
　　　　　The Officers Commanding,
　　　　　　　4th Brigade R.F.A.
　　　　　　　9th Brigade R.F.A.
　　　　　　　13th Brigade R.F.A.
　　　　　　　61st Howitzer Battery R.F.A.

　　　　　　　In continuation of my No.770-R.A.(L), dated the 28th June 1915, the following extract from MEERUT Division Operation Order No.41 dated the 27th June 1915, is forwarded for information and such action as necessary:-

　　　x x x　　　　　　　　　　　　　　x x x

EXTENSION OF　1. The MEERUT Division front is extended to the
FRONTAGE &　　North to the ESTAIRES-LA BASSEE Road exclusive.
AREA.　　　　　The boundaries of the billeting area are modified:-
　　　　　　　　On the North to the line LA BASSEE Road-RUE du
　　　　　　　　BOIS junction exclusive- Road junction S 4 a 8'9.
　　　　　　　　exclusive- our present line at St. VAAST.
　　　　　　　　On the South to l'EPINETTE-RUE du BOIS Road
　　　　　　　　junction inclusive- thence through K 17 a 10'3-
　　　　　　　　K 10 d 3'5 and R 32 c 7'0, where the old boundary
　　　　　　　　is resumed.

RELIEFS.　　　2. BAREILLY Brigade on the night 28th/29th June
　　　　　　　　will take over from GARHWAL Brigade the front from
　　　　　　　　BOND STREET Communication trench exclusive to the
　　　　　　　　ORCHARD Post ~~xxxxxxxxxxxxxxxxxxxxxxxxxxxxxxxxxxxxxxxxxxxxxx~~ inclusive, and from FEROZEPORE
　　　　　　　　Brigade from ORCHARD Post exclusive to the
　　　　　　　　ESTAIRES-LA BASSEE Road exclusive.

　　　x x x　　　　　　　　　　　　　　x x x

　　　　　　　　The G.O.C. BAREILLY Brigade will take over
　　　　　　　　command of his new front as soon as the relief is
　　　　　　　　completed. Brigade Headquarters in farm at
　　　　　　　　M 32 d 7'8.

　　　x x x　　　　　　　　　　　　　　x x x

DIVISIONAL　　5. The G.O.C. GARHWAL Brigade will detail one
RESERVE.　　　British and two Indian Battalions as Divisional
　　　　　　　　Reserve, to be billetted in LES LOBES R 28 d and
　　　　　　　　R 34 b. State of readiness- two hours notice.

　　　x x x　　　　　　　　　　　　　　x x x

NOTE:- BAREILLY BRIGADE FRONT:- LA BASSEE ROAD to BOND STREET
　　　　Communication trench(exclusive)(S 9 d 9'5 approx:).
　　　　This will be held by 3 battalions in the front line.

　　　　GARHWAL BRIGADE FRONT:- BOND STREET Communication
　　　　trench(inclusive)(S 9 d 9'5 approx:) to R.5.
　　　　This will be held by 2 battalions in the front line.

2.

DEHRA DUN BRIGADE FRONT:- R.5. to QUINQUE RUE.
This will be held by 3 battalions in the front line as at
present.

Major R.A.
Brigade Major, Royal Artillery,
MEERUT DIVISION.

SECRET.

APPENDIX 284

TACTICAL PROGRESS REPORT
28th June 1915.

1(a) ACTION BY OUR OWN ARTILLERY.

9.15.a.m. 44th Battery fired at farm S.E. of P.18 in retaliation for fire on our trenches.
2.50.p.m. 20th Battery fired some H.E. at houses at M.14 by request of 21st Infantry Brigade.
4.15.p.m. 44th Battery fired 6 rounds at working party carrying planks in trench between P.15 and P.14.
6.30.p.m. 44th Battery fired 2 salvoes at supposed field gun position near N.24; the trenches in front of SAVOY having been shelled from that direction.
During the afternoon the 20th Battery fired a few rounds at German front trench P.14 - N.14 to show points to Battery of 52nd Brigade taking over from them.

(b) ACTION BY HOSTILE ARTILLERY.

9.30.a.m. 15.c.m. howitzer shelled vicinity X 24 a 8'8. French Observation ladder in Orchard struck.
11.a.m. 10.5.c.m. howitzer shelled our trenches in vicinity of M.9.
15.c.m. howitzer shelled vicinity DEAD COW FARM(S 14 d).
11.15.a.m. to 12.15.p.m. 15.c.m. howitzer shelled PRINCES ROAD- hitting house near S 14 d 9'3.
11.30.a.m. 21.c.m.(?) howitzer shelled support trenches East of INDIAN VILLAGE.
3.15.p.m. 15.c.m. howitzer again shelled vicinity of DEAD COW FARM.
3.30.p.m. 15.c.m. howitzer shelled cross roads RUE du BOIS - RUE de l'EPINETTE for about half an hour.
5.30.p.m. 10.5.c.m. howitzer shelled INDIAN VILLAGE from direction of VIOLAINES.
6.15.p.m. 77.mm. shelled trenches near R.15 from direction of DISTILLERY.
77.mm. shelled our trenches at various times during the day.

2. INFORMATION.

MOVEMENTS:- 4.p.m. Germans seen carrying planks between P.13 and P.14.

R. K. Lynch-Staunton.
Major R.A.

Brigade Major, Royal Artillery,
MEERUT DIVISION.

1st BRIGADE R.G.A. OPERATING ON OUR FRONT REPORT:-

12.10.p.m. 8th Siege engaged A 6 a 7'7 which was reported very active by 4th Brigade R.G.A. shelling S 15 d and neighbourhood.
5.35.p.m. This battery again active and taken on by 8th Siege in conjunction with 48th Heavy Battery.

4th BRIGADE R.G.A. OPERATING ON OUR FRONT REPORT:-

OUR ACTIVITY:- 10.9.a.m. 48th engaged S 12 b 5'0 in reply to 77.mm. active on PONT LOGY.
10.42.a.m. 110th engaged S 30 b 2'3 active.
11.17.a.m. 48th shelled trench K.7 to X.5. O.O. 13th H.B. observed the first 4 or 5 rounds- 2 of which fell into the side of the trench.
11.25.a.m. 110th engaged the howitzer occupying A 6 a 7'7.
12.12.p.m. 110th engaged LORGIES.
12.42.p.m. 48th fired at S 23 c 9'1 and S 29 b 4'4.
3.16.p.m. 110th took on A 6 a 7'7 again.
5.25.p.m. 48th in conjunction with 8th Siege fired at the "Canon in Residence".
6.7.p.m. 110th engaged S 23 b 8'3 active.

P.T.O.

HOSTILE ACTIVITY:-
8.30.a.m. S 23 c 9'1 on our trenches.
9.18.a.m. DISTILLERY 77.mm. active.
10.21.a.m. Howitzer from BEAU PUITS on S 21 c 3'7.
11.50.a.m. Howitzer on S 15, possibly "Canon in Residence" or a near neighbour.
4.p.m. DISTILLERY 77.mm. active.
6.10.p.m. S 23 c active.

SECRET.

TACTICAL PROGRESS REPORT
29th June 1915.

1. (a) ACTION BY OUR OWN ARTILLERY.

10.a.m. 44th Battery fired one salvo at probable 77.mm. position near N.24. Two 77.mm. shell burst 300 yards in front of battery just after this.
11.15.a.m. 20th Battery registered FERME de TOULOTTE and fired a few rounds into M.13 (a likely O.P.)- two direct hits.
1.10.p.m. 44th Battery fired 30 rounds in conjunction with 60 pr. Battery on RUE du MARAIS.
1.p.m. 2nd Battery fired 4 rounds in retaliation for hostile shelling of our trenches.
1.30.p.m. 8th Battery fired at working party in a trench W. of FERME COUR d'AVOUE.
3.30.p.m. 19th Battery fired a few rounds on trenches in vicinity of X.30 in conjunction with Siege Battery firing on that locality.
5.40.p.m. 28th Battery fired 12 rounds on enemy's trenches about X.27 - X.28 in reply to rifle fire on our aeroplane.
61st Howitzer Battery registered R.18.

(b) ACTION BY HOSTILE ARTILLERY.

10.30.p.m. 28th June 1915. One 21.c.m. howitzer shell fell near LA COUTURE.
During the morning the enemy shelled Orchard at M.9. and support trenches in rear with field guns.
A little howitzer and 77.mm. shelling our trenches during the day.
5.45.p.m. Some heavy shell passed over ROUGE CROIX.
5.55.p.m. Heavy burst of fire on our right probably GIVENCHY (for about 5 or 10 minutes).

2. INFORMATION.

21st Infantry Brigade report trench mortar at N.14.

A quiet day.

Lieut R.A.

for Brigade Major, Royal Artillery,
MEERUT DIVISION.

1st BRIGADE R.G.A. OPERATING ON OUR FRONT REPORT:-

6.15.p.m. 28th June 1915. 8th Siege Battery engaged battery active at S 23 d 1'4- 4 rounds fired, hostile battery ceased firing.
8.20.p.m. 28th June 1915. 8th Siege Battery engaged active battery A 6 b 3'0- 4 rounds fired- light too bad to observe.
1.p.m. 29th June 1915. Batteries active from HAUTE POMMEREAU. 8th Siege Battery fired 5 rounds at the Ranging House as it was impossible to spot active batteries.

4th BRIGADE R.G.A. OPERATING ON OUR FRONT REPORT :-

48th Heavy Battery engaged S 24 b 0'10, S 23 c 9'1, T 14 c 10'0, T 1 d 3'5, S 23 c 9'8, S 30 central.
109th Heavy Battery engaged S 6 b 10'3, T 8 a 8'8, T 1 b 9'5, T 2 c 8'5 and LA CLIQUETERIE.
110th Heavy Battery engaged A 6 a 7'7, T 19 d 4'6.
Enemy howitzer E. of BOIS du BIEZ active on S 10 at 4.10.p.m.

APPENDIX 286

No.779-R.A.(L).   Headquarters Divisional Artillery,
                                              MEERUT DIVISION.

                                              30th June 1915.

CONFIDENTIAL.
        To,

            The Officer Commanding,
                    7th Battery R.F.A.

        One section of your battery is to go into action tonight, after dark, in relief of one section of 28th Battery R.F.A. in B X 23 b 8'5.   Traffic routes to be adhered to.
Remaining two sections will probably relieve the remainder of 28th Battery tomorrow night but further instructions will issue. Registration will be taken over from 28th Battery, but as the occupation of this position is only temporary, no drastic structional alterations are to be made to the position, or damage done thereto.
New position for your battery will be prepared by you during course of next few days, ready for occupation on return of 28th Battery from rest.

                                              Major R.A.

                              Brigade Major, Royal Artillery,
                                        MEERUT DIVISION.

    Addressed to O.C. 7th Battery R.F.A.(direct).
    Copies for information to:- O.C. 4th Brigade R.F.A.
                                 O.C. 9th Brigade R.F.A.

No. 780-R.A.(L).   Headquarters Divisional Artillery,
                                        MEERUT DIVISION.

SECRET.   30th June 1915.

MEERUT   DIVISIONAL   ARTILLERY,   APPENDIX 287

INSTRUCTIONS FOR ARTILLERY RELIEFS ON 30th JUNE 1915.

9th Brigade R.F.A.

At 3.p.m.(approx) 19th and 20th Batteries now supporting IV Corps area will be relieved by two batteries of 52nd Brigade (IX Division).

At 3.30.p.m.(approx) 19th Battery will take over support of "D" Sub-section (GARHWAL BRIGADE) from 13th Brigade battery. 20th Battery will take over the support of "A" Sub-section (DEHRA DUN BRIGADE), as a temporary measure, from a 13th Brigade battery.

At 11.p.m. One section of 28th Battery-on IX Division front-will be relieved by one section of 7th Battery (from St FLORIS).

4th Brigade R.F.A.

At 3.p.m.(approx) 14th Battery and 66th Battery take over support of "B" and "C" Sub-sections (DEHRA DUN BRIGADE) from 2 batteries 13th Brigade R.F.A.

At 11.p.m.(approx) One section of 7th Battery will relieve One section of 28th Battery (IX Division front).

13th Brigade R.F.A.

At 3.30.p.m.(approx) the three batteries of 13th Brigade will be relieved of the support of the DEHRA DUN and GARHWAL BRIGADE front by batteries of the 9th and 4th Brigades (see above), and will in their turn proceed to relieve the three batteries of the 18th Brigade R.F.A.(LAHORE DIVISIONAL ARTILLERY) of the support of the BAREILLY BRIGADE front.

GROUPING:-

Following will therefore be the "Grouping" of batteries with Infantry Brigades, after above reliefs have taken place:-

DEHRA DUN BRIGADE. "A" Sub-section *20th Battery of IX Bde.
                    "B" Sub-section) 14th and 66th Batteries
                    "C" Sub-section) of IV Brigade.

GARHWAL BRIGADE.   "D" Sub-section 19th Battery of IX Bde.

Bareilly
~~DEHRA DUN~~ BRIGADE. "E" Sub-section 44th Battery)   of
                    "F" Sub-section 8th Battery)   XIII
                    "G" Sub-section 2nd Battery)Brigade.

* Temporary measure only, pending relief of 28th Battery IX Brigade (now on IX Division front) by 7th Battery of IV Brigade.

LIASONS:-

Each battery will establish communication with Infantry Battalion holding the sub-section which it is ordered to support.

COMMUNICATIONS:-

Artillery Brigade Commanders should ask Infantry Brigade Signal Officers to establish communication with their respective Headquarters.

P.T.O.

HEADQUARTERS:-

    IV Brigade R.F.A..............CROIX BARBEE M 26 c 5'1
                                                    (temporarily).

    IX Brigade R.F.A..............X 17 d.

    XIII Brigade R.F.A............R 29 d.

                                                    R.M. Lynch-Staunton.
                                                               Major R.A.

                                  Brigade Major, Royal Artillery,
                                          MEERUT DIVISION.

To:-

    The General Staff, MEERUT Division.

    The G.O.C. DEHRA DUN Brigade.

    The G.O.C. GARHWAL Brigade,

    The G.O.C. BAREILLY Brigade.

    The G.O.C., R.A., LAHORE DIVISION.

    G.O.C., R.A., IX Division.

    The G.O.C. RA VII Division.

    The O.C. 4th Brigade R.F.A.

    The O.C. 9th Brigade R.F.A.

    The O.C. 13th Brigade R.F.A.

    The O.C. 61st Howitzer Battery R.F.A.

    The O.C. MEERUT Divisional Ammunition Column.

APPENDIX 288

SECRET.

TACTICAL PROGRESS REPORT
30th June 1915.

1(a) ACTION BY OUR OWN ARTILLERY.

2.p.m. 8th Battery registered new front, relieving a battery of LAHORE Divisional Artillery.
4.p.m. 19th Battery registered trenches from FERME du BOIS to V.2.
5.45.p.m. and 6.20.p.m. 14th Battery fired 5 rounds on working party between Q.11 and Q.15.
6.p.m. 44th Battery registered new front relieving a battery of LAHORE Divisional Artillery.

(b) ACTION BY HOSTILE ARTILLERY.

77.mm. shelled trenches in front of FERME du BOIS and COUR d'AVOUE at irregular intervals during the night 29th/30th. This was being continued at 8.5.a.m.
3.20.p.m. Heavy howitzer shelled in direction of 48th Heavy Battery.
3.55.p.m. 15.c.m. howitzer shelled vicinity X 24 b(4 rounds).
4.p.m. 15.c.m. howitzers shelled INDIAN VILLAGE from direction of VIOLAINES.
5.45.p.m. 77.mm. shelled neighbourhood of RITZ.
6.30.p.m. 15.c.m. howitzer shelled our trenches about S 21 b.

2. INFORMATION.

RELIEFS:- During the day the following Artillery reliefs were carried out:-
13th Brigade R.F.A. relieved 18th Brigade R.F.A.(LAHORE Divisional Artillery) in support of the BAREILLY Brigade front.
4th Brigade R.F.A.(less one battery) and 20th Battery(9th Brigade) took over the support of the DEHRA DUN Brigade front.
19th Battery(9th Brigade R.F.A.) took over support of the GARHWAL Brigade front("D" Sub-section).

R H Lynch-Staunton
Major R.A.

Brigade Major, Royal Artillery,
MEERUT DIVISION.

4th BRIGADE R.G.A. OPERATING ON OUR FRONT REPORT:-

48th Heavy Battery engaged S 18 c 10'0, S 6 d 7'4, S 7 a 9'2.
109th Heavy Battery engaged B 7 b 0'6 as 28th Heavy Battery was shelled from that direction. Several crumps were fired at O.P's in answer to this.
110th Heavy Battery engaged T 25 c 8'5, S 24 central, A 6 a 7'7, S 23 c 9'1, T 19 d 7'7, T 19 a 2'2 and DISTILLERY 77.mm.

www.ingramcontent.com/pod-product-compliance
Lightning Source LLC
Chambersburg PA
CBHW081425160426
43193CB00013B/2193